ESSENTIAL

BUSINESS STUDIES
for you

KEY NOTES

Robert Dransfield

STANLEY THORNES

First published in 2000 by
Stanley Thornes (Publishers) Ltd
Ellenborough House
Wellington Street
Cheltenham
GL50 1YW
UK

A catalogue record for this book is available from The British Library.

ISBN 0 7487 5495 4

00 01 02 03 04/10 9 8 7 6 5 4 3 2 1

Diagrams by Steve Ballinger, cartoons by Shaun Williams
Typeset by Paul Manning
Printed and bound in Great Britain by Redwood Books, Trowbridge, Wiltshire

Contents

Matching Grids

The following grids show how sections of this book relate to particular GCSE syllabuses.

OCR (Midland Examining Group)

Syllabus unit	Section of this book				
	1	2	3	4	5
The External Environment of the Business	◆				
Business Structure and Organisation		◆			
Business Behaviour			◆		
People in Business				◆	
Aiding and Controlling Business Activity					◆

Southern Examining Group (SEG)

Syllabus unit	Section of this book				
	1	2	3	4	5
The External Environment of the Business	◆				◆
Business Structure and Organisation		◆			◆
Business Behaviour			◆		◆
People in Business				◆	

Northern Examination and Assessment Board (NEAB)

Syllabus unit	Section of this book				
	1	2	3	4	5
The External Environment of the Business	◆				◆
Ownership and Control of Business		◆			◆
The Aims and Objectives of Business	◆			◆	
The Management of People within a Business				◆	
Finance			◆		
Production			◆		
Marketing			◆		

Welsh Joint Committee

Syllabus unit	Section of this book				
	1	2	3	4	5
The Business Environment	◆				◆
Structure, Organisation and Control		◆			◆
Business Objectives	◆			◆	
Rules and Relationships				◆	
Business Finance			◆		
Production and Marketing			◆		

EdExcel Foundation

Syllabus unit	Section of this book				
	1	2	3	4	5
Business Activity and the Environment	◆				
Structure, Organisation and Control of Business		◆			◆
Rules, Relationships and Management in Business				◆	
Sources, Uses and Management of Finance			◆		
Production and Marketing Strategies			◆		

Scottish Qualification Authority (SQA)

Syllabus unit	Section of this book				
	1	2	3	4	5
What is Business?	◆	◆	◆	◆	◆
How do Businesses Develop and Perform?	◆	◆	◆	◆	◆
What Resources do Businesses Use?	◆	◆	◆	◆	◆
How are Businesses managed?	◆	◆	◆	◆	◆

Getting Your Revision Right

After working on your Business Studies course for two years and having successfully completed your coursework, you will naturally want to make sure that your final revision will get you the grade that you deserve.

This book is designed to help you quickly revise all the key areas of the Business Studies GCSE. If you learn all of the sections in this book you should have the knowledge to tackle all the questions in your examination with confidence.

The book is based on the same type of visual approach used in modern business organisations, where everyone needs to grasp what is happening in the business as quickly as possible. Ideas are communicated in simple charts and diagrams using a 'three-minute management' approach. In the same way, all the diagrams and features in this book are designed to allow you to grasp the main points within three minutes.

Applying your knowledge

In the examination you will be expected to apply the knowledge that you have learnt to case studies and other questions. So here are some simple tips to bear in mind:

1 **Read the question and think carefully about what are you being asked to do.**
2 **Think how you can use business knowledge and ideas to help you answer the question.**
3 **Use your business knowledge to answer the question. The question will usually relate to a fictional business. Make sure that you relate your answer to the business in the question.**

Levels of response

In Business Studies many of your answers will be marked using a 'levels of response' approach.

At a simple level you will simply give facts and information which you have learnt. This will not score many marks.

To score higher marks, you need to be able to apply your knowledge and understanding to the case material that you are presented with. For example, the question may ask you to apply your knowledge of the marketing mix to a *particular* business, rather than just to talk about the marketing mix as it would apply to *any* business.

Some questions will ask you to go even further. For example, you may be asked to make recommendations and to evaluate various policies and activities. In order to make recommendations, you need to show that you have considered alternatives. You need to show *why* you made a particular decision (i.e. show the evidence which led you to that decision). You may also want to examine the short-term and long-term implications of a particular choice or decision.

So, in using this guide, remember that knowledge on its own is not enough. Success at Business Studies GCSE is concerned with *how you use what you know.*

About this book

This revision book is designed to be used alongside the textbook *Business Studies for You*, by David Needham and Robert Dransfield, also available from Stanley Thornes. You will see that it has been broken up into five sections. At the end of each section is a set of short questions (*Show That You Know It!*) designed to help you to check that you have learnt the essential sections of knowledge.

Each section is sub-divided using headings like the following:

> **Demonstrate understanding of economic activity in helping to satisfy the needs of society.**

These sub-headings are very important. In particular, look at the first two or three words which tell you what is expected of you, for example:

◆ *Demonstrate understanding…*
◆ *Show an appreciation…*
◆ *Classify…*
◆ *Identify the key features…*
◆ *Explain the importance of…*

During your revision, ask yourself, 'Can I **demonstrate** (*show*) that I understand....X?', 'Can I **classify** (*put into groups*)… Y?' – and so on.

If you feel that you can do these things then you can be confident that you can answer any question asked of you covered under that particular sub-heading.

At the end of the book you will find two test papers for you to test yourself in exam conditions. The answers to these and to the short questions are given in the final section.

A word of warning…

Don't leave your revision to the night before the exam. If you want to learn the information in this book, you will have to build it into a carefully designed revision programme. You will also need to study, and practise answering, past questions from your examining board to familiarise yourself with the best ways to apply your knowledge.

1.1 THE ECONOMIC ENVIRONMENT

Demonstrate understanding of economic activity in helping to satisfy the needs of society.

Economic activity is concerned with adding value to products.

For example, a **roll of paper** can be turned into a more valuable **book**:

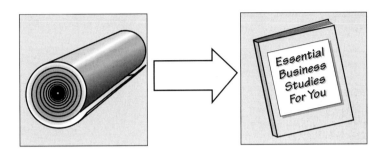

Economic activity creates goods to satisfy people's wants and needs. These include:

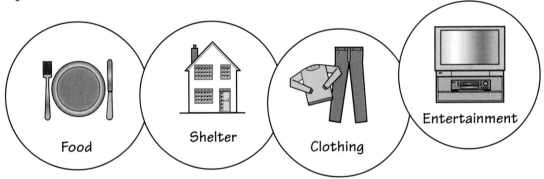

Food   Shelter   Clothing   Entertainment

Economic activity is all the processes that go into making goods by adding value to partly finished products.

There can be many stages in adding value to a product. Taking the example of oil:

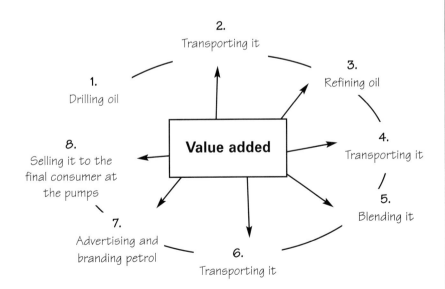

Value added

1. Drilling oil
2. Transporting it
3. Refining oil
4. Transporting it
5. Blending it
6. Transporting it
7. Advertising and branding petrol
8. Selling it to the final consumer at the pumps

1.1 THE ECONOMIC ENVIRONMENT (CONTD.)

Show an appreciation of the basic problems of scarcity, choice and allocation of resources.

A resource like:

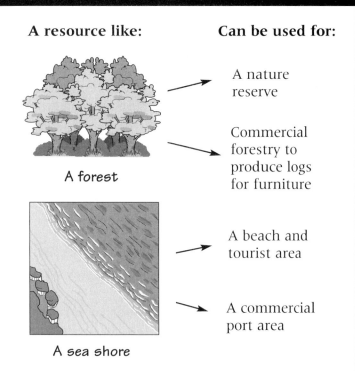

A forest

A sea shore

Can be used for:

A nature reserve

Commercial forestry to produce logs for furniture

A beach and tourist area

A commercial port area

Most resources are scarce.

This means there are not enough of them to produce all the goods required to satisfy consumers' wants and needs.

Individuals, businesses and society at large have to make choices about how best to use the resources at their disposal.

A resource used for one purpose will not be available for another. Resources need to be allocated to given purposes.

You can allocate resources into producing:

◆ more guns or more butter
◆ more consumer goods or more machines

In each case you have to make a choice. You can't have everything that you want!

"Every time I make a choice I have to give up the next best thing!"

1.1 THE ECONOMIC ENVIRONMENT (CONTD.)

Demonstrate an understanding of the concept of opportunity cost.

Opportunity cost is the sacrifice that is made when you make a choice. It is the sacrifice of the next-best alternative.

The opportunity cost to the government of building a hospital may be a school – the next best thing it could have done with its money.

Either...   Or...

Granby Casualty Hospital

Granby School

Businesses need to consider opportunity cost all the time – the real cost of buying a machine might be that they are not able to employ ten more workers.

The opportunity cost of having an employee working on one project is the contribution he or she could have been making to another project in that time.

If John buys a new pair of trousers…

…he may not be able to buy the CD that was his next-best choice.

"I had to pay so much in tax last year that I couldn't afford a new Jaguar!"

1.1 THE ECONOMIC ENVIRONMENT (CONTD.)

Classify firms into primary, secondary and tertiary sectors.

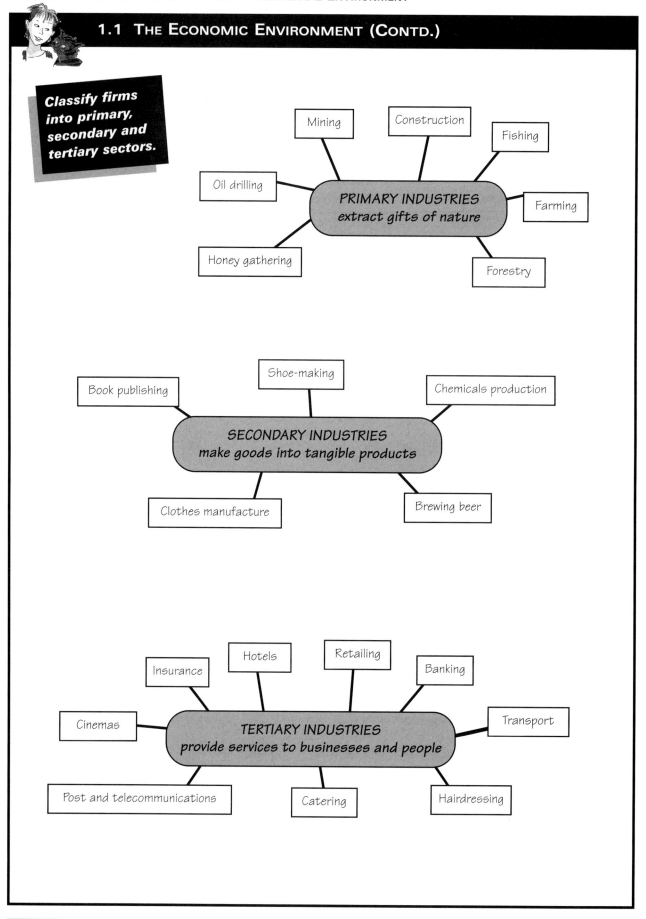

Mining

Construction

Fishing

Oil drilling

PRIMARY INDUSTRIES
extract gifts of nature

Farming

Honey gathering

Forestry

Book publishing

Shoe-making

Chemicals production

SECONDARY INDUSTRIES
make goods into tangible products

Clothes manufacture

Brewing beer

Hotels

Retailing

Insurance

Banking

Cinemas

TERTIARY INDUSTRIES
provide services to businesses and people

Transport

Post and telecommunications

Catering

Hairdressing

1.1 THE ECONOMIC ENVIRONMENT (CONTD.)

Show understanding of the changing importance of the primary, secondary and tertiary sectors – particularly the impact of the growth of the tertiary sector on UK business.

Over time, the UK economy has experienced a number of 'waves of activity' as society has developed:

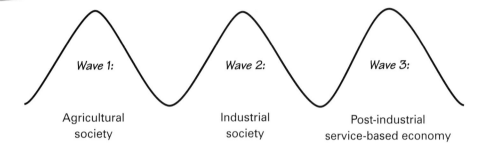

Wave 1: Agricultural society

Wave 2: Industrial society

Wave 3: Post-industrial service-based economy

Numbers employed in the primary sector have been falling for some time.

For example, today there are just over 200,000 people employed in agriculture, but these workers are highly productive because of the advanced machinery and equipment they use. Numbers employed in mining and fishing have also fallen steadily.

Employment in agriculture is declining

Numbers of employees in the secondary sector have also been falling:

Numbers Employed in the Secondary Sector		
Manufacturing		**Construction**
Metals, minerals and mineral products ⬇		Building ⬇ ⬆
Chemicals and artificial fibres ⬇		Civil engineering ⬇ ⬆
Engineering ⬇		
Food, drink and tobacco ⬇ ⬆		
Textiles, footwear, clothing and leather goods ⬇		

⬇ = Job losses in many firms   ⬆ = Job gains in some firms

1.1 THE ECONOMIC ENVIRONMENT (CONTD.)

Primary, secondary and tertiary sectors, Contd.

Banking – a tertiary-sector activity

Numbers in the tertiary sector have grown and will continue to grow across the sector as a whole.

Numbers Employed in the Tertiary Sector		
Retailing	↑ ↓	Banking and finance	↑ ↓
Distribution	↑ ↓	Public administration	↑ ↓
Hotels and catering	↑ ↓	Education	↑ ↓
Post and telecommunications	↑ ↓	Health services	↑ ↓

↓ = Job losses in many firms   ↑ = Job gains in some firms

"Some of today's small technology firms will be global businesses by the end of the decade."

Modern service-sector businesses are very consumer-focused – i.e. they work hard to build a strong relationship with consumers.

Service organisations tend to have a strong Information Technology focus – they employ 'knowledge workers', i.e. intelligent people who use Information Technology and who work closely with customers and work colleagues.

1.1 THE ECONOMIC ENVIRONMENT (CONTD.)

Identify the key features of, and changes in, the structure of the UK economy.

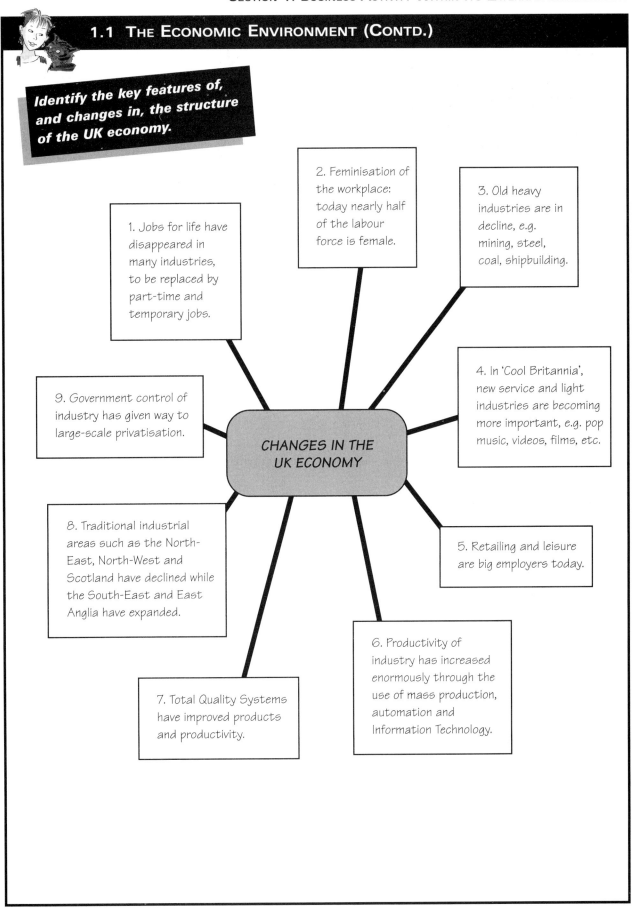

1. Jobs for life have disappeared in many industries, to be replaced by part-time and temporary jobs.

2. Feminisation of the workplace: today nearly half of the labour force is female.

3. Old heavy industries are in decline, e.g. mining, steel, coal, shipbuilding.

4. In 'Cool Britannia', new service and light industries are becoming more important, e.g. pop music, videos, films, etc.

5. Retailing and leisure are big employers today.

6. Productivity of industry has increased enormously through the use of mass production, automation and Information Technology.

7. Total Quality Systems have improved products and productivity.

8. Traditional industrial areas such as the North-East, North-West and Scotland have declined while the South-East and East Anglia have expanded.

9. Government control of industry has given way to large-scale privatisation.

CHANGES IN THE UK ECONOMY

1.2 THE BUSINESS

The European Union is a market of 350 million people. It is mainly made up of advanced economies with a ready market for the sorts of goods and services produced in the UK.

The UK joined the European Union in 1973. In the early days member states concentrated on developing economic ties. More recently they have been concerned with strengthening economic, political, social and monetary ties.

Left: The 15 member states of the European Union

As a member state, the UK must abide by EU regulations governing economic, social and environmental policy. The next step may be the harmonisation of tax systems.

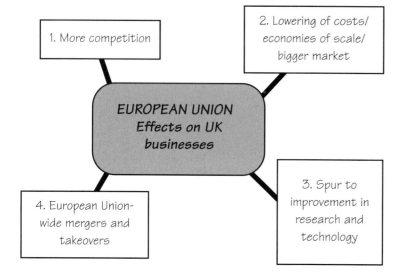

1. More competition

2. Lowering of costs/ economies of scale/ bigger market

EUROPEAN UNION Effects on UK businesses

3. Spur to improvement in research and technology

4. European Union-wide mergers and takeovers

"There's too much interference from Brussels, if you ask me – foreigners should keep their nose out of our business!"

1.2 THE BUSINESS (CONTD.)

Explain the importance of the Single European Market.

Advantages of EU membership:

◆ Gives firms a home market of 350 million people
◆ No customs duties between countries
◆ Increased competition between firms, who now benefit from huge economies of scale
◆ Creation of a single currency means less uncertainty about future economic and trading conditions (once the UK signs up)

Within the Single European Market created in 1992, firms can take advantage of four important freedoms:

1.
Freedom of movement of people (labour)

2.
Freedom of movement of goods

THE FOUR FREEDOMS

4.
Freedom of movement of services

3.
Freedom of movement of capital (finance)

1.2 THE BUSINESS (CONTD.)

Identify and demonstrate understanding of the importance of business objectives (e.g. growth, profitability, wealth creation, market share and survival) and their interrelationship.

The end that an individual or organisation works towards is their **objective**.

Your objective is to achieve an A* in your Business Studies course!

What are the objectives of businesses?

Objective →

Profit
All businesses need to consider profit – without profit businesses will be unable to achieve their other objectives.

Profit is measured by:

Total Revenue – Total Cost

Objective →

Market share
Having the biggest share of the market helps to drive down costs.

Market share is measured by:

$$\frac{\text{Market Share of Company A}}{\text{Market Share of Nearest Rival}}$$

Objective →

Growth
Increased size enables firms to benefit from economies of scale.

Growth is measured by growth in:

◆ Turnover
◆ Profits
◆ Return On Capital Employed (ROCE)

Objective →

Wealth creation
To create wealth for stakeholders in the company

Wealth creation is measured by:

◆ Returns to shareholders
◆ Increases in wages and salaries of employees

Objective →

Survival
To stay in business and keep adapting to changing market conditions

Survival is measured by the length of time a company stays in the market place

1.2 THE BUSINESS (CONTD.)

Explain the roles of different groups involved in business: owners, producers, consumers, employees, government and taxpayers.

Employees
E.g. people who work at Shell Head Office, traders in oil, lorry drivers and people who work on oilrigs. All expect good pay and conditions in return for their labour.

Owners
Shareholders put up the equity capital of the business and receive rewards in the form of dividends. Shareholders can vote at the Annual General Meeting.

THE SHELL OIL COMPANY IS A PRODUCER OF OIL, GAS, AND CHEMICAL PRODUCTS

Consumers
Include businesses, e.g. industrial users of chemicals, and private consumers – e.g. purchasers of fuel in Shell garages.

Government
Creates the laws and regulatory framework in which oil companies operate. Government policy influences the state of the economy. Businesses must pay taxes, e.g. corporation tax to the government

Taxpayers
Businesses collect tax for the government, e.g. income tax and VAT. Businesses themselves are also taxpayers.

1.2 THE BUSINESS (CONTD.)

Explain the differing aims of private- and public-sector organisations, and demonstrate awareness of the changes that have taken place in the UK economy.

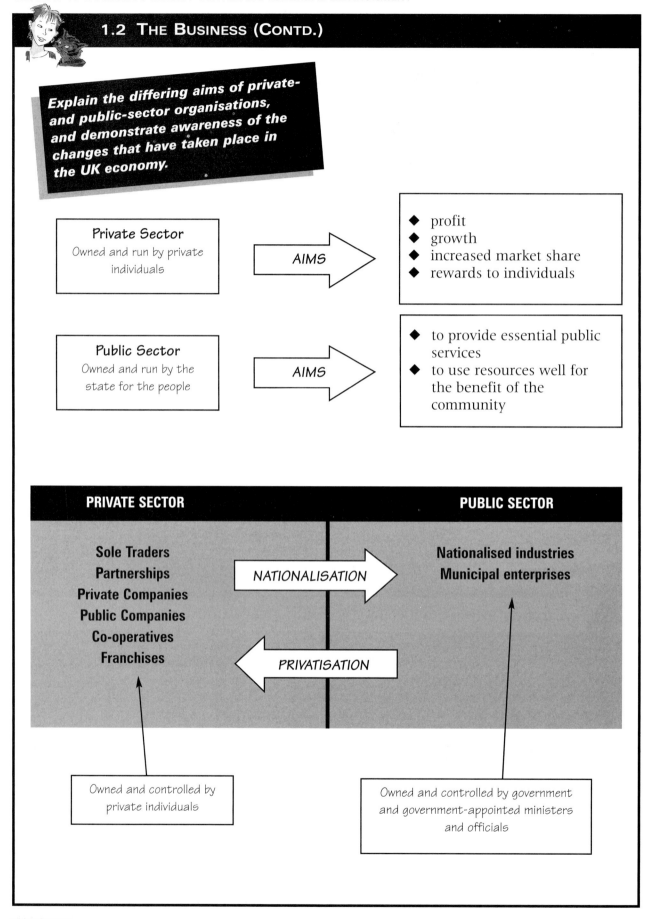

Private Sector		
Owned and run by private individuals	AIMS	◆ profit ◆ growth ◆ increased market share ◆ rewards to individuals

Public Sector		
Owned and run by the state for the people	AIMS	◆ to provide essential public services ◆ to use resources well for the benefit of the community

PRIVATE SECTOR

Sole Traders
Partnerships
Private Companies
Public Companies
Co-operatives
Franchises

NATIONALISATION

PUBLIC SECTOR

Nationalised industries
Municipal enterprises

PRIVATISATION

Owned and controlled by private individuals

Owned and controlled by government and government-appointed ministers and officials

1.2 THE BUSINESS (CONTD.)

Identify and give examples of recent changes in private and public ownership.

"Privatisation is good – privately owned businesses have to make a profit or they go bust!"

Many nationalised industries and other government run businesses have been privatised.

Examples of privatised industries now include:

British Airways

British Rail

The coal industry

British Telecom

Privatised industries are owned by shareholders and are subject to much greater levels of competition than the former public corporations.

Shareholders in privatised industries can vote on important issues at the company's AGM. They can even vote to replace the directors.

1.3 BUSINESS IN ITS ENVIRONMENT

Explain how government policy influences decisions within local, national and international contexts and explain how businesses may react.

Government creates rules which business must comply with at different levels. For example:

Rio and Kyoto International Treaties on Environment
(to reduce harmful levels of pollution)

Influence

European Union-wide regulations

Influence

UK government legislation

Influences

Local government rules and requirements
for businesses

The government taxes and spends money:

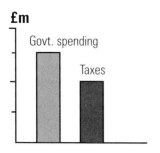

A **deficit budget** pumps money into the economy, helping to create business optimism and jobs

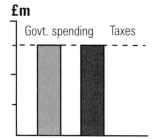

A **balanced budget** keeps the economy on an even keel

Government may also tax richer people at higher rates than others in order to distribute wealth more equally.

Government can also discourage anti-social activities by, for example:

◆ taxes on smoking
◆ taxes and other penalties on firms that create pollution

Government can subsidise 'desirable' behaviour, e.g. award grants to firms to introduce anti-pollution equipment, or to create jobs in areas of high unemployment.

1.3 BUSINESS IN ITS ENVIRONMENT (CONTD.)

Explain the different ways of measuring the size of a business and select and justify appropriate measures of size in given circumstances.

How do you measure the size of a business?

The answer depends on the nature of the business or industry. If it is a **labour-intensive** industry – e.g. hairdressing – then the number of employees may be relevant. If it is **capital-intensive** – e.g. brewing beer – then turnover may be more relevant.

Measures of size include:

◆ number of branches or business units
◆ value of output
◆ number of employees
◆ capital assets of the company
◆ value of sales
◆ volume of output
◆ range of activities

Describe and explain ways in which business responds to the needs of consumers and the actions of competitors.

E.g. United States retail chain Wal-Mart says 'The consumer is king'

Marketing – find out what consumers want and deliver it

How consumer- focused organisations respond to the needs of customers

Ensure product matches customer requirements

Get the 4 Ps right: product, place, price and promotion

Consider price and non-price factors in marketing of products

Always keep one jump ahead of the competition

How competitor-focused organisations respond to the actions of market rivals

E.g. John Lewis organisation claims to be 'never knowingly undersold'

Marketing mix must match or exceed that of competitor.

1.3 BUSINESS IN ITS ENVIRONMENT (CONTD.)

Show awareness of the ways business can respond to the needs of the community and environment.

Business In The Community is an organisation set up by the Prince of Wales in partnership with business leaders to encourage business involvement in community projects.

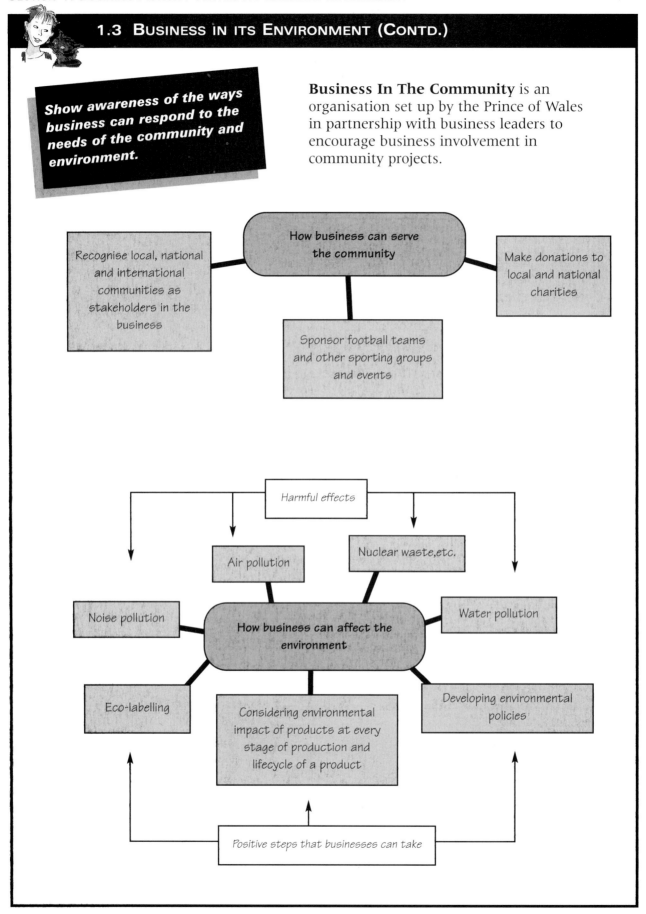

How business can serve the community

- Recognise local, national and international communities as stakeholders in the business
- Sponsor football teams and other sporting groups and events
- Make donations to local and national charities

Harmful effects

How business can affect the environment

- Noise pollution
- Air pollution
- Nuclear waste, etc.
- Water pollution

Positive steps that businesses can take

- Eco-labelling
- Considering environmental impact of products at every stage of production and lifecycle of a product
- Developing environmental policies

SHOW THAT YOU KNOW IT!

1 What is **economic activity**?

2 How can economic activity help to meet consumer needs?

3 Why are goods said to be **scarce**?

4 What is the **opportunity cost** to you of revising for your Business Studies GCSE exam?

5 What might the real cost be to a business of investing in a new factory?

6 Classify the following into **primary, secondary** and **tertiary** occupations. Show why each fits into a particular category:

Oil driller   Police officer
Insurance clerk   Bank manager
Gold miner   Shoemaker
Building worker   Farm labourer
Shop worker   Film maker
Professional footballer Textile worker
Marketing director   Fisherman

7 Which sector of the economy employs the highest numbers of people in advanced industrial economies? Why?

8 Why are service sector organisations so **consumer-focused**?

9 Does the **feminisation** of the labour force mean that women are doing the best paid work?

10 What factors have led to the increased productivity of manufacturing industry in the UK in recent years?

11 Which areas of the country have seen regional economic decline in recent years? Why?

12 How large a market is the **European Union**? When did the UK join?

13 In what ways does the existence of the European Union act as a spur to the improvement of UK business?

14 What are the advantages to business of having a **Single European Currency**, the Euro?

15 What are the **Four Freedoms**?

16 Outline and explain four major business objectives.

17 Explain how you could measure profit, market share, growth, and wealth creation by a business.

18 Explain the roles of the following in business: consumers, employees, government, taxpayers and **one** other group.

19 What is the difference between the **public** and the **private** sector of the economy?

20 List **six** types of business that exist in the private sector, and **two** in the public sector.

21 What is meant by **privatisation**? List six industries that were privatised in the last twenty years of the twentieth century.

22 What is a **deficit budget** and why might a government set one?

23 Explain five ways of measuring the size of businesses.

24 Why might some businesses be influenced more by the actions of consumers than by their competitors?

25 Why might some businesses be influenced more by the actions of competitors than by consumers?

2.1 OWNERSHIP AND INTERNAL ORGANISATION

Explain or discuss the appropriateness of the legal and internal structures a firm adopts to its objectives and to its potential for growth.

A business needs to consider the most appropriate legal form for its existence – in particular, whether or not to become a company.

◆ A company exists as a **corporate body** in law. Once it is established, other people must deal with the company as a legal entity rather than with the individual owners of the company.

◆ Owners of a company have **limited liability**. This means that individual shareholders or other forms of owners of the company can only lose at a maximum what they have invested in the company – their own private possessions cannot be seized to pay off the debts of the company.

◆ **Having company status enables the organisation to raise a lot of share capital.** This brings in funds for expansion.

Describe the main features and give examples of sole traders.

In a sole trader business, there is one owner. A sole trader can employ other people and still have sole trader status.

Examples:

◆ plumber
◆ electrician
◆ window-cleaner
◆ home hairdresser
◆ freelance journalist

Many hairdressers are sole traders

Sole trader advantages	Sole trader disadvantages
+ Cheap to set up + Makes all own decisions + No complicated paperwork to set up + Owner takes all profit	− No limited liability − Many responsibilities for one person − No access to partners or share capital − Tax returns are time-consuming and complicated to fill in

2.1 OWNERSHIP AND INTERNAL ORGANISATION (CONTD.)

Describe the main features and give examples of partnerships.

Examples:
- solicitors
- vets
- doctors
- accountants

Main features of a partnership:
- Must have 2–20 partners
- Set up by a **Deed of Partnership** signed in presence of a solicitor
- Deed sets out who will do what, how profits will be shared, etc.

Partnership advantages	Partnership disadvantages
+ More capital than sole trader + More expertise and division of labour + Partners can take holidays + New ideas come into the business + Partners take profits for themselves + Plenty of scope for decision-making	− Partners have to consult each other − Disagreements − Complicated legal work when one partner pulls out − No limited liability − Still only limited capital compared to a company

Describe the main features of a private company.

Main features of a private company:
- Must have two or more **shareholders**
- Must register a **Memorandum and Articles of Association** with the Registrar of Companies
- Must have a **registered office**

Private company advantages	Private company disadvantages
+ Access to more capital from shareholders + Shareholders have limited liability + Company is separate in law from individuals who own it + Less paperwork than a PLC + Can employ specialist managers	− Not as much capital as public limited company − Profits have to be shared among shareholders − More paperwork than sole trader/partners − Often disagreements between managers/ directors

The private limited company is owned by shareholders who are represented by a Board of Directors. They are often family-owned businesses. Mars is one of the best examples of a private company in this country. Private companies have **Ltd** after their name.

2.1 OWNERSHIP AND INTERNAL ORGANISATION (CONTD.)

Describe the main features of public companies.

Main features of a public company:

◆ Like a private company, a public company must be registered with the **Registrar of Companies**, and this involves lengthy paperwork
◆ Shares are traded on the **Stock Exchange** and **Unlisted Securities Market**
◆ The company is owned by the **shareholders**

Public company advantages	Public company disadvantages
+ Can raise large sums of money from sale of shares and debentures + Employs specialist managers + Extensive economies of scale + Shareholders have limited liability + Shares can be given to employees to encourage commitment and improvements in performance	− Has to pay dividend to shareholders and interest to dividend holders – a drain on capital for investment − Easy to lose control of company through takeover, particularly when share prices fall − May become too large, leading to diseconomies of scale, e.g. managerial inefficiencies − Loss of personal touch

Describe the main features and give examples of public corporations.

Main features of a public corporation:

◆ Owned by the government for the people
◆ Public corporations were a popular way of running nationalised industries from 1946 until 1979, when Margaret Thatcher started widescale privatisation. They were established by Act of Parliament
◆ Chairperson chosen by government minister is responsible for day-to-day administration
◆ Run by professional managers

◆ Activities can be scrutinised by committees of MPs, and ministers questioned in Parliament
◆ Decisions can be politically influenced, e.g. not to close down a mine in an area of high unemployment
◆ Complaints investigated by Consumer Council

The best-known example of a public corporation is the **BBC**.

2.1 OWNERSHIP AND INTERNAL ORGANISATION (CONTD.)

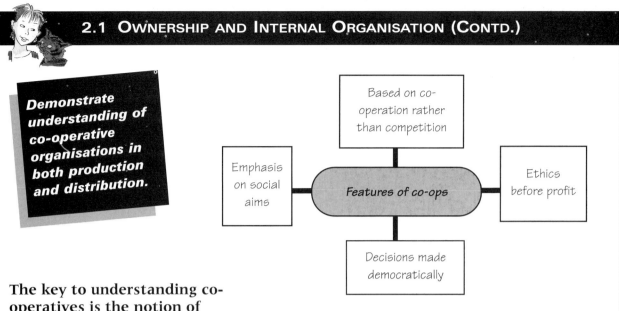

Demonstrate understanding of co-operative organisations in both production and distribution.

Features of co-ops
- Based on co-operation rather than competition
- Emphasis on social aims
- Ethics before profit
- Decisions made democratically

The key to understanding co-operatives is the notion of MUTUALITY.

◆ Co-operatives set out to provide **mutual** (shared) benefits to their members – i.e. the **co-operators**

◆ The key point of difference between a co-operative and some of its rivals is the co-op emphasis on **ethical trading** – e.g. co-ops will not buy goods from firms that exploit their own workers

◆ Individual shoppers can attend meetings of their local co-op by buying a £1 share. Co-ops aim to pass on their profits to shoppers, e.g. in lower prices and quality items

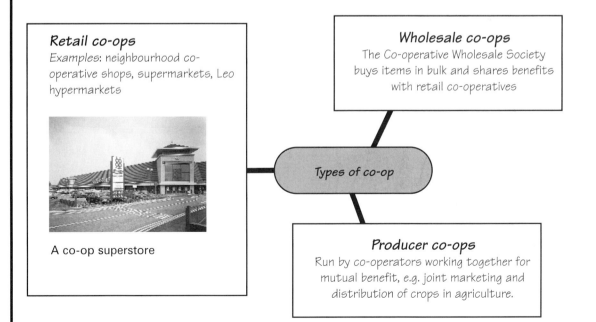

Retail co-ops
Examples: neighbourhood co-operative shops, supermarkets, Leo hypermarkets

A co-op superstore

Wholesale co-ops
The Co-operative Wholesale Society buys items in bulk and shares benefits with retail co-operatives

Types of co-op

Producer co-ops
Run by co-operators working together for mutual benefit, e.g. joint marketing and distribution of crops in agriculture.

2.1 OWNERSHIP AND INTERNAL ORGANISATION (CONTD.)

Explain the differences between the three basic types of business organisation in terms of objectives, control, sources of finance and distribution of profits.

Organisation	Objectives	Control	Sources of finance	Distribution of profits
Sole trader	Profit, survival, growth	By the owner	Owners' capital, overdraft, loans, grants, mortgage, venture capital, profit	All to the owner (after paying interest on money borrowed)
Partnership	Profit, to run a professional service, survival, growth, increased market share	By the partners	Partners' capital, overdraft, loans, grants, mortgage, venture capital, sleeping partners, profit	Between partners (after paying interest on money borrowed)
Private company (Ltd)	Profit, wealth creation, survival, growth, increased market share	By the Board of Directors or managers	Share capital, overdraft, loans, mortgage, venture capital, debentures, profit	Between shareholders (after interest paid on money borrowed)
Public company (PLC)	Profit, wealth creation, survival, growth, increased market share	By the Board of Directors and managers	Share capital, overdraft, loans, mortgage, venture capital, debentures, profit	Between shareholders (after interest paid on money borrowed)
Co-operative	Mutual benefits, social objectives, profit, survival	By management committee	Members' capital, loans, mortgages, etc., reinvested profits	Among members, also passed on to consumers as lower prices
Public corporation	Return on capital equivalent to private sector, social objectives	Major decisions by government minister, day-to-day control by chairperson and management	Government funds, borrowing from financial institutions, profits	Surpluses can be returned to Treasury

2.1 OWNERSHIP AND INTERNAL ORGANISATION (CONTD.)

Demonstrate understanding of the role of government in business activity and of the agencies through which it operates.

How government affects business activity:

◆ **Government departments** carry out important functions, e.g. Inland Revenue collects Income Tax
◆ **Public corporations** play a key role in national life, e.g. BBC is responsible for public service broadcasting
◆ **Training and Enterprise Councils** (TECs) receive government funding and are responsible for implementing local training initiatives, e.g. the New Deal

Creates the 'rules of the game' – the legal and regulatory framework for business activity

Can be directly involved in business activity, e.g. collects licence fee for BBC and appoints Director General

Government

Uses taxes to build the infrastructure of the economy, e.g. roads, transport, education

Seeks to control economic activity – in a recession may raise taxes; in a boom may lower taxes

Appoints **regulators** to control aspects of privatised industries such as price rises

Demonstrate understanding and give examples of franchising.

How franchising works

A firm with a good idea sells the right to use that idea in a particular area.

Examples:

Dial-A-Pizza, Dunkin Donuts, McDonalds, The Body Shop, Super Rod. Coca-Cola franchises its bottling operations in many countries.

Franchisor gets	Franchisee gets
+ A lump sum from franchisee	+ A nationally known name
+ A share of the franchisee's profits	+ A tried and tested business idea
+ Publicity from having a nationwide network	+ Support and advice
+ Equipment, supplies and training from franchisee	+ Equipment, materials and supplies

The franchisee is likely to work very hard as they are working for themselves as well as for the franchisor.

2.1 OWNERSHIP AND INTERNAL ORGANISATION (CONTD.)

Draw, explain and interpret simple organisational charts.

In the illustration above, the organisation is structured into a number of functions with functional managers. There are **four** levels in the hierarchy. The **span of control** of the Managing Director is four functional managers. The span of control of the production supervisor is 64 production workers.

◆ The Managing Director has a **narrow** span of control.
◆ The Production Supervisor has a **broad** span of control (possibly because all the production workers are doing similar and tightly specified work).

The fewer the number of levels in the hierarchy, the broader the span of control.

'Tall' and 'flat' organisations

When planning organisational structure, companies need to think about **communication**:

◆ In **flat** organisations, communication between the top and bottom should be more direct.
◆ In a **tall** organisation each subordinate has a more direct relationship with a superior.

"I run a flat organisation alright — it's flat broke!"

2.2 FINANCING BUSINESS ACTIVITIES

Understand the use and management of finance (e.g. capitalisation, Balance Sheet analysis, cash flow forecasting).

Businesses need finance to service their activities – e.g. to buy goods for resale, to pay for premises, to purchase machinery, etc.

Businesses need to manage this finance so that they have enough of the right type of finance at the right time.

Capitalisation is concerned with how a business uses capital to fund its activities.

Different types of business are capitalised in different ways:

Capitalisation	
Sole traders and partnerships	*Companies*
Largely owners' capital and some borrowing, added to by profits in the course of time	Shareholders contribute capital plus borrowing and profits over time

It is important to examine the ratio of owners' capital to borrowing. A business that borrows large sums will be faced with heavy interest repayments.

◆ The **Balance Sheet** is a snapshot taken at a particular moment in time. It shows:

Liabilities	*Assets*
What the business owes	What the business owns or is owed

◆ It is important to understand how the Balance Sheet is made up because this shows whether the business has enough of particular types of assets to meet its liabilities.

Cash flow forecasting

Cash is the most **liquid** of all assets. You must have enough cash coming in to meet the immediate needs of the business. This requires careful management.

2.2 FINANCING BUSINESS ACTIVITIES (CONTD.)

Show an appreciation of the need for short- and long-term finance.

Identify internal and external sources of finance for both private- and public-sector organisations.

Short- and long-term finance

◆ **Short-term finance** is designed to be paid back quickly whereas long-term finance may be paid back over many years, e.g. 25 or more for a mortgage. Short-term finance may be needed to buy petrol for a taxi firm, pay wages in all types of businesses, buy stock on credit in a retailer, etc.

◆ **Long-term finance** is needed for the fixed assets of a company, e.g. buildings, machinery, fixtures and fittings.

Internal finance

Private sector	Public sector
◆ Owners' capital ◆ Shareholders' capital	◆ Funds already in organisation

External finance

Private sector	Public sector
◆ Short-term trade credit (i.e. not having to pay for goods for 1 month, 3 months, etc.) ◆ Medium-term hire purchase, i.e. borrowing from finance house to purchase an asset – e.g. car, only owned when final payment is made ◆ Venture capital – money borrowed from a venture capital firm such as 3i ◆ Medium-term bank loan ◆ Short-term overdraft – being allowed to spend more than you have in your bank account ◆ Long-term mortgage – being able to borrow against the collateral of a building or land ◆ Medium-term leasing of equipment (hired but never owned)	◆ Grants from central government ◆ Loans ◆ Hire purchase ◆ Leasing ◆ Trade credit

2.2 FINANCING BUSINESS ACTIVITIES (CONTD.)

Explain the factors which affect the method of finance chosen by a particular business, e.g. nature of business and project, size of business, cost of finance and risk involved.

Frankie and Cleo visit the bank manager to discuss a business loan

The type of finance a business chooses depends on several different factors:

Factor	Method of finance
Nature of business	**Manufacturing businesses** need finance to buy raw materials (e.g. trade credit); to pay wages (e.g. overdraft); to buy buildings (e.g. mortgage); to buy machinery and equipment (e.g. loans, hire purchase). **Retailing businesses** need finance to buy stock for resale (e.g. trade credit) to pay wages (overdraft), fixtures and fittings (loans, etc.)
Nature of project	For **on-going projects**, businesses require long-term investment, e.g. new production line (loans, other long-term finance). For **day-to-day projects**, businesses need short-term finance, e.g. purchase of supplies.
Size of business	**Small businesses** are financed internally through owners' capital, externally through venture capital, overdrafts, loans, mortgage. **Large businesses** have access to wider range of sources of funds – e.g. internally from shareholders, externally from City of London; can also issue debentures.
Cost of finance	Usually borrowing costs are **higher** for **small** businesses than for **large** ones. Overdraft is a cheap way of borrowing, so long as the borrower keeps within the terms of the arranged overdraft. The greater the number of shares sold, the lower unit cost per share. Mortgages and long-term loans are costly.
Risk	The higher the **risk**, the higher the **cost** of finance. Mortgages are risky because **collateral** (i.e. security) is required. Leasing also involves a longer-term commitment.

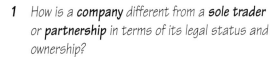

SHOW THAT YOU KNOW IT!

1   How is a **company** different from a **sole trader** or **partnership** in terms of its legal status and ownership?

2   Why might it be more advantageous to set up a small shop as a sole trader rather than as a partnership?

3   Describe the main features of a **private company**.

4   Give examples of **public limited companies** and explain **three** major advantages that they have relative to private limited companies.

5   Give an example of a **public corporation** and explain how it is set up and run.

6   How is a public corporation **accountable** to consumers and the general public?

7   Explain **four** main features of **co-operatives** in retailing.

8   Who has **control** over the activities of a partnership? What are its main sources of finance? How will its profits be distributed?

9   What are the most common **objectives** of private and public companies?

10 What are the chief sources of **finance** for (**a**) a sole trader, and (**b**) a PLC?

11 What type of organisation would make a **surplus** rather than a profit?

12 Describe **five** major roles for the government in controlling and influencing business activity.

13 Give **two** examples of organisations that operate through **franchising**, and explain the advantages of taking out a franchise rather than setting up a company of your own.

14 Draw an **organisation chart** showing **four** levels of hierarchy, with each member of the organisation having a span of control of **three** people.

15 What are the advantages of a **flat** over a **tall** organisation?

16 How might sole traders and partnerships raise their **starting capital**?

17 What does a **Balance Sheet** show?

18 Why is it important to draw up a **cash flow forecast**?

19 What is the difference between **short-term** and **long-term finance**?

20 What are the main sources of **internal finance** for **private-sector** organisations?

21 What are the main sources of **external finance** for **private-sector** organisations?

22 What are the main sources of **external finance** for organisations in the **public sector**?

23 How might the nature of a **business** influence the methods of finance used?

24 How might the nature of a **project** influence the methods of finance used?

25 Why might an **overdraft** prove to be cheaper than a **loan** as a method of finance?

3.1 MARKETING

Show how a business finds out about markets for its product/s using internal and published information, market surveys and test markets.

Marketing is the anticipation, and identification of consumer wants and needs in order to meet these needs, and to make a profit.

Primary and secondary research

◆ **Primary** research is original research which you carry out to find out information, e.g. by interviewing people or using a questionnaire.
◆ **Secondary** research involves using someone else's published research.

Internal
Analyse company records, sales records, records of complaint

Published information
Examine publications which tell you about consumption and buying patterns, e.g. MINTEL, Acorn

Methods of market research

Test marketing
Testing out a good or service in a small section of the market and analysing the results, e.g. in a particular TV region

Market surveys
Conducting surveys (or hiring a market research company to do it for you)

Sources of market research data

MINTEL is a market research organisation that investigates lots of different markets. Mintel surveys can be purchased.

ACORN is a way of classifying the UK into housing areas which share common features. Marketers can then target their marketing at these areas using postcodes.

The Annual Family Expenditure Survey finds out what families in the UK spend their money on and how this changes over time.

3.1 MARKETING (CONTD.)

Conduct field and desk research using appropriate methods.

When carrying out research it is important to be clear about your objectives.

Think about:

◆ **piloting** research on a small scale first
◆ how you select your sample. A **random sample** is one in which each person belonging to the wider population has an equal chance of being selected. **Quota sampling** ensures that sections of the population are sampled who have the same characteristics as the target market

Analyse, present, interpret and use information.

In examining market research information you need to draw out the key points – e.g. what sorts of people want to buy the product, how much are they prepared to pay, etc. This information can be set out in tables and charts.

Recommendations and **conclusions** can be drawn out about how the company should act on this information.

Show how markets may be segmented according to age, socio-economic grouping, location, price, quality or purpose.

A segment is a part of the overall market made up of people with similar characteristics.

Identifying segments enables the marketer to target marketing activities more effectively.

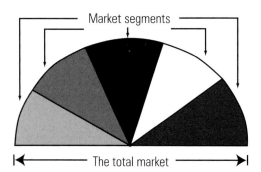

3.1 MARKETING (CONTD.)

Market segments Contd.

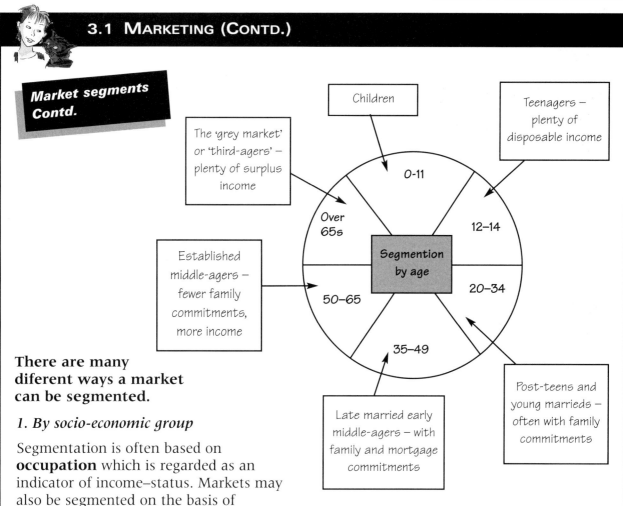

The 'grey market' or 'third-agers' – plenty of surplus income

Children

Teenagers – plenty of disposable income

Established middle-agers – fewer family commitments, more income

Segmention by age

Over 65s

0-11

12-14

50-65

20-34

35-49

Late married early middle-agers – with family and mortgage commitments

Post-teens and young marrieds – often with family commitments

There are many diferent ways a market can be segmented.

1. By socio-economic group

Segmentation is often based on **occupation** which is regarded as an indicator of income–status. Markets may also be segmented on the basis of **housing area**.

Membership of a particular socio-economic group is seen as a measure of spending power, and is often used to group newspaper readers, car-owners, etc, in categories such as **A, B, C, C2, D**. These denote sections of society ranging from 'wealthy professionals' to 'low income/unemployed'.

2. By location

People who live in different areas may have very different characteristics, e.g. consider the contrasting lifestyles of urban and rural households. Also regional differences may be significant: people may be more figure- and health-conscious in the South East than in the Midlands. Again, the country can be broken into regional segments, or ACORN classifications can be used (see page 31).

3. By price, quality or purpose

- ◆ **'Upmarket'** customers tend to look for higher price and better quality
- ◆ **'Downmarket'** customers tend to look for lower price and lower quality

Purpose is also significant. For example, a car may be bought for business or pleasure. Different groups have different requirements, e.g. for a business customer, performance and reliability may be more important than looks.

3.1 MARKETING (CONTD.)

Select and justify a method of segmentation appropriate to given circumstances.

Example 1

For a biscuit company producing a low-price biscuit, **socio-economic** segmentation may be relevant. For example, it may make sense to target advertising at C2/D/E groupings by advertising during a soap opera like *Coronation Street*. Of course, **price** segmentation is also relevant.

"Businesses nowadays take a big interest in the youth market – that's because young people have got buying power!"

Example 2

A firm produces chairlifts for the elderly and infirm. It therefore uses **age-based** segmentation, targeting its marketing activities at magazines read by pensioners – because this is the best way of reaching this target group.

Demonstrate understanding of the product life cycle.

Nearly all products go through a life cycle – although the length of each phase will vary.

Advertising is important:

◆ prior to the launch
◆ during the growth period
◆ to stop maturity setting in too early

During the period of decline it may not be worth spending a lot of money on advertising and promotion unless you want to relaunch the product completely.

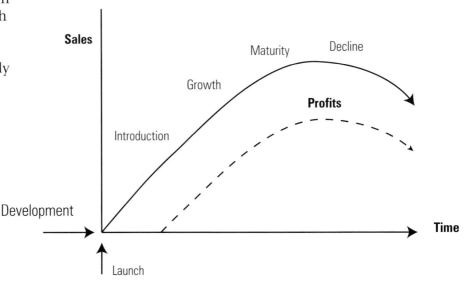

3.2 PRODUCTION

Understand production and marketing objectives and related strategies.

Production and marketing objectives should be closely related – i.e. they should be focused on creating 'quality products' that meet customer requirements.

Quality means 'fitness for purpose' – i.e. the product does what customers expect it to do.

In the past many UK companies were accused of being too **production-oriented** (focused on what they were good at making) rather than being **marketing-oriented** (making what consumers wanted to buy).

Explain, with examples, job, batch, process and flow methods of production.

1. Job production

Job production = 'one-off' production'

Examples:

◆ Building a house
◆ Cutting hair
◆ Knitting a sweater

Job production advantages	Job production disadvantages
+ Allows attention to detail + Allows focus on the one job/one customer + Product meets individual specifications	− Costly because no mass production − Problem if customer is not happy with job or can't pay

3.2 PRODUCTION (CONTD.)

Production processes Contd.

2. Batch production

Identical items are produced in a batch. Different products are produced in separate batches, often using the same equipment which is modified and/or reset.

In a modern bakery, a batch of cakes can be followed by a batch of bread rolls, then a batch of biscuits

Batch production advantages	Batch production disadvantages
+ Care and attention can be given to each batch + Provides variety for employees + Enables same employees and equipment to be used for variety of purposes, e.g. a batch of cakes can be followed by a batch of biscuits or bread rolls	− Cost and time of resetting equipment

3. Process production

Often a number of processes are required to produce one product. Each process can be carried out using specialist machinery and labour. In many factories workers will take partly finished goods out of store, process them and then return them to stores.

Process production advantages	Process production disadvantages
+ Each process is carried out by specialists + Everyone knows exactly what is expected of them.	− If mistakes occur it is not always clear who was responsible − Waste of time as goods in process of being made keep being taken out and put back in store

3.2 PRODUCTION (CONTD.)

Production processes Contd.

4. Flow production

This is the modern method of mass production. Products flow down a line along which all the processes are completed. The production line is often computer-controlled.

Flow production advantages	Flow production disadvantages
+ Mass production, economies of scale Once line is set up products just keep flowing along it + Can run 24 hours a day + Use of automation and computer checking systems	− Eliminates need for human skills (dehumanising) − If mistakes occur can lead to vast quantities of wasted products , e.g. Coca Cola poisoning in Belgium in 1999 − Does not allow customisation of products

Select and justify the right production method for different circumstances.

Production method	Circumstances
Job production	◆ Where product must meet individual customer specifications ◆ Where attention to detail is important ◆ Where the product is a non-standard item
Batch production	◆ Where equipment and labour can be adapted to meet different requirements ◆ Where there is a range of similar but different orders ◆ Where demand does not justify continuous flow production
Process production	◆ Where production consists of a set of distinct stages/processes ◆ Where the organisation has specialist equipment/labour processes for each process ◆ Where each process requires specialist skills
Flow production	◆ Where demand is very high ◆ Where the company has the space and resources to set up a flow ◆ Where mass production results in significantly lower unit costs

3.2 PRODUCTION (CONTD.)

State and explain costs a business may incur in production.

A business incurs costs in the production and selling process.

The greater the level of output or sales, the higher the costs will be – including costs of **labour** (wages), **capital** (interest), **raw materials**, etc.

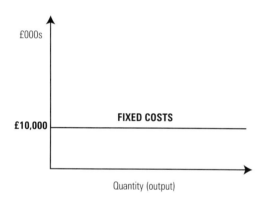

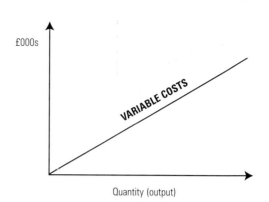

◆ **Fixed costs** do not vary with level of output. E.g. a firm may have to pay same sum for the rent of its premises, whether it produces 0 units or 1 million.

  Examples: rent, rates, interest on loans, etc.

◆ **Variable costs** increase with output. The more you produce, the higher your total variable cost.

  Examples: wages, fuel and energy costs, raw materials, etc.

Classify costs and show understanding of fixed and variable costs, and direct and indirect costs.

Direct costs

Direct costs an be directly associated with the production of a particular product – e.g. the cost of the mince that goes into a tin of factory-produced Spaghetti Bolognese. Direct costs increase with output.

Indirect costs (overheads)

Indirect costs cannot be directly associated with a particular product line as they may go into the production of several products. For example, the lighting and heating in a factory may be used on several product lines. Indirect costs need to be 'apportioned' to products in a sensible way – e.g. if half of the factory's output is Cannelloni, then 50% of heating and lighting costs can be apportioned to the Cannelloni product line.

3.2 PRODUCTION (CONTD.)

Explain, interpret and use simple break-even models.

The break-even point (BEP) shows the output that a business needs to achieve in order to cover its total cost.

To calculate the break-even point:

1 Calculate the unit contribution (Selling Price *less* Variable Cost)
2 Divide the Fixed Costs by the Unit Contribution:

$$\text{Break-even point} = \frac{\text{Fixed Costs}}{\text{Contribution}}$$

Example
A firm has Fixed Costs of £80,000.
Goods are sold at £12 per unit and the Variable Cost is £8 per unit.
Unit Contribution = £4 (£12 – £8)
Fixed Costs = £80,000
$$\frac{80,000}{4} = 20,000 \text{ units of output}$$

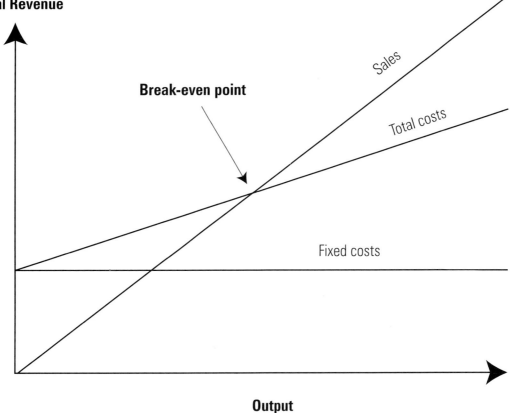

Total, Fixed and Variable Cost and Total Revenue

Sales

Total costs

Break-even point

Fixed costs

Output

3.2 PRODUCTION (CONTD.)

Demonstrate understanding of advantages and disadvantages associated with the scale of production and give examples.

Products can be produced on a large or small scale.

Economies of scale are the advantages of producing on a large scale, enabling a firm to produce at low average costs per unit. As the number of units produced by a firm increases, the cost per unit decreases.

Disadvantage of small-scale production: unit costs are higher.

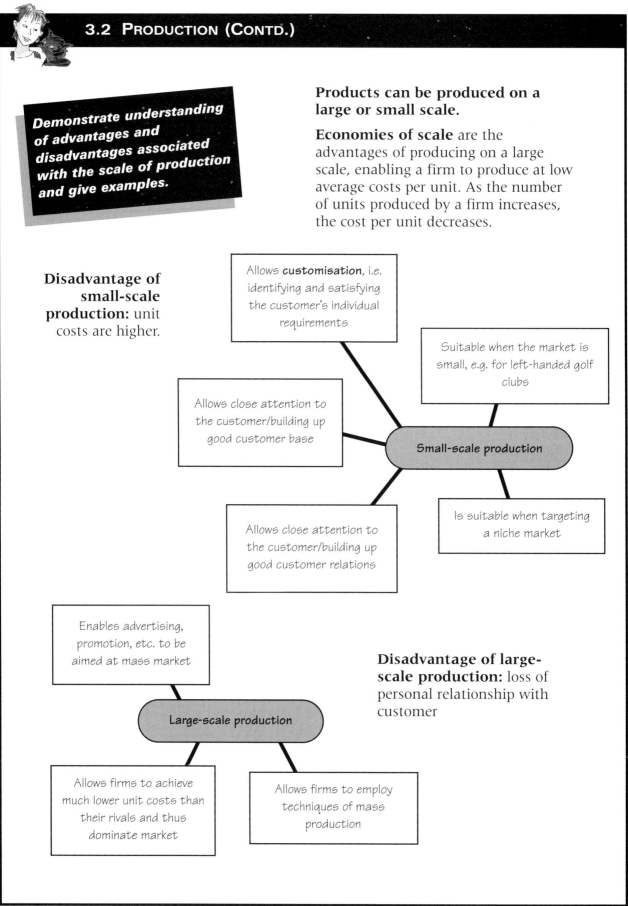

Allows **customisation**, i.e. identifying and satisfying the customer's individual requirements

Suitable when the market is small, e.g. for left-handed golf clubs

Allows close attention to the customer/building up good customer base

Small-scale production

Allows close attention to the customer/building up good customer relations

Is suitable when targeting a niche market

Enables advertising, promotion, etc. to be aimed at mass market

Large-scale production

Disadvantage of large-scale production: loss of personal relationship with customer

Allows firms to achieve much lower unit costs than their rivals and thus dominate market

Allows firms to employ techniques of mass production

3.2 PRODUCTION (CONTD.)

Demonstrate understanding of economies of scale and give examples.

There are a number of benefits of scale which can help firms reduce their unit costs.

◆ **Internal** economies of scale stem from size of an individual firm.

◆ **External** economies of scale benefit all the firms in an industry – e.g. the development of new roads to a particular location, the improvement of research facilities, etc.

"Big firms can buy their supplies more cheaply!"

Economies of scale	Business benefits
Trading economies	Buying and selling goods in large volumes enables firms to benefit from discounts and reduced transportation costs per unit
Marketing economies	Large-scale advertising campaigns can reach millions of homes
Technical economies	Business activities can be better organised, e.g. firms can use bigger and better machinery, combine processes together, employ specialist labour and machinery
Managerial economies	Specialist managers can be employed to improve efficiency and drive down costs
Risk-spreading economies	A variety of products and product lines can be produced to reduce vulnerability to changing market conditions
Financial economies	Large firms can borrow money more cheaply and raise capital more effectively on the Stock Exchange

3.3 MARKETING THE PRODUCT

Identify, explain and give examples of the four main elements of the marketing mix.

The Marketing Mix: Product, Placement, Price and Promotion

The Marketing Mix

1. The Product

Without a **product** there is nothing for a firm to market. Most products contain the following four elements:

What does the product look like?

What does the product do?

1. Design

What makes the product different?

4, Range
Many firms ofer a range of products aimed at different segments of the market, e.g. a razor manufacturer might offer a disposable razor, a long-lasting razor, Lady Shave, etc.

THE PRODUCT

2, Name
A key ingredient, can be worth billions to a company, e.g. 'Coca-Cola', 'Mars', 'Hoover'

3. Packaging
◆ Protects productfrom damage
◆ Keeps product fresh
◆ Gives instructions and details
◆ Also useful for promotion and advertising

MANUFACTURERS			
Channel A	Channel B	Channel C	Channel D

Company warehouse

Wholesaler

Retailers

Company outlets

Retailer

CONSUMERS

2. Placement (channels of distribution)

Length of channel varies.

Key
A   Direct selling
B   Company controls channels
C   Traditional distribution pattern
D   Widely used today.

3.3 MARKETING THE PRODUCT (CONTD.)

The Marketing Mix Contd.

3. Price

Pricing strategies and methods include:

Price strategy	Method	Objective
Penetration	Low price	To enter a new market to get a good initial share. E.g. with the arrival of digital television, Sky Digital penetrated the market with a very low starting price
Discounting	Reducing prices	Cutting prices in order to beat the competition
Destroyer	Low price	Setting the price so low that competitors are forced out of the market e.g. the media tycoon Rupert Murdoch sold *The Times* at a giveaway price to try and destroy the market of *The Daily Telegraph* and *The Independent*.
Skimming/creaming	Starting at a higher price	Starting by selling a good at a high price to people who have a strong desire to buy – then progressively reducing the price to sell to new groups of consumers
Premium	High price	Selling goods at a higher price than rivals to create a quality image for the product/brand

3.3 MARKETING THE PRODUCT (CONTD.)

The Marketing Mix Contd.

4. Promotion

Promotion includes advertising, media selection and point-of-sale promotion. It uses a variety of ways of bringing goods and services to the attention of customers.

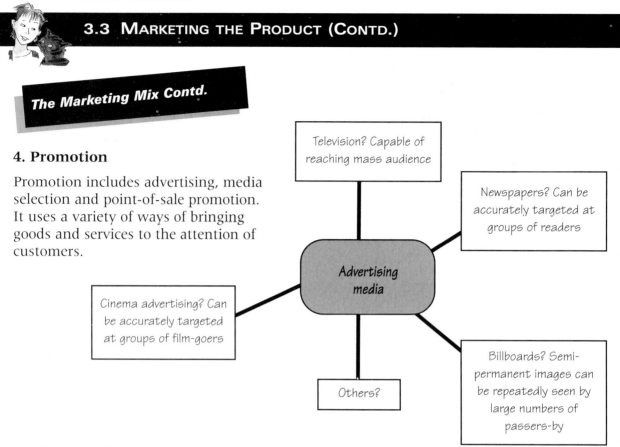

Television? Capable of reaching mass audience

Newspapers? Can be accurately targeted at groups of readers

Advertising media

Cinema advertising? Can be accurately targeted at groups of film-goers

Others?

Billboards? Semi-permanent images can be repeatedly seen by large numbers of passers-by

Media selection considerations

When choosing advertising media, the goal is to achieve the maximum penetration of an appropriate target audience with the greatest impact and the best return for each £ spent.

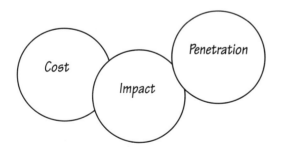

Cost

Impact

Penetration

Three key factors to consider when selecting media for a promotional campaign

Point-of-sale-promotion

Bringing the good or service to the attention of the buyer in the place where it is typically bought – e.g. petrol vouchers and stamps given away free at filling stations.

"The best promotion is the one that creates the most impact per pound spent."

3.4 PLANNING, CONTROLLING AND REPORTING

Show understanding of the importance of cash flow and forecasting.

Businesses need to manage their cash flow effectively. Cash is the 'oil' that enables a business to run smoothly: without enough cash coming in the business seizes up.

The **cash flow cycle** is similar to the water cycle in nature. Funds are transformed from a **liquid resource** – cash – into other resources such as property, equipment and stocks. These resources generate income from customers which eventually flows back into the business in the form of cash.

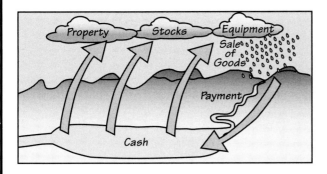

The cash flow cycle

"Cash!! Lovely stuff!!'

The cash flow statement

A **cashflow statement** sets out a business's proposed expenditure and income over time and shows its net cash balance. It is a forecast, i.e. a **budget**.

Example			
	Period 1	Period 2	Period 2
Sales	10,000	10,000	10,000
Purchases	6,000	6,000	10,000
Net cash flow	4,000	4,000	0
Cash carried forward	4,000	8,000	8,000

3.4 PLANNING, CONTROLLING AND REPORTING (CONTD.)

Define profit and calculate gross and net profit.

Profit is the surplus which a business accrues from its trading or manufacturing activities over a period of time.

Gross profit

For a trading company:

Gross profit = Sales – Cost of Sales
(i.e. cost of purchasing items for resale)

For a manufacturing company:

Gross Profit = Sales – Cost of Manufactured Goods

Trading Account of Fred Jones for year ended 31/12/2001

	£	£
Sales		30,000
Less Cost of Sales		
Opening Stock	9,000	
Add Purchases	18,000	
	27,000	
Less Closing Stock	12,800	14,200
Gross Profit		**15,800**

3.4 PLANNING, CONTROLLING AND REPORTING (CONTD.)

Gross and net profit Contd.

Net Profit

Net profit is the final profit after the expenses of running the business have been deducted.

Profit and Loss Account of Fred Jones
for year ended 31/12/99

	£	£
Gross Profit		15,800
Less Expenses		
Electricity	500	
Insurance	50	
Salaries	5,000	
Advertising	50	5,600
Net Profit		**10,200**

Explain the importance of profit as a reward for risk-taking.

People who put money into a business could invest in other things, e.g. in a Building Society. What they could earn in this next-best line is the opportunity cost of using the money in the chosen way.

As a part-owner of a business, you are taking a risk: you may make less money by investing in the business than by investing in the Building Society. Putting money into a company therefore needs to be rewarded. Profit acts as an incentive to take risks. The greater the chance of making a profit, the more likely that people will be willing to take a risk.

3.4 PLANNING, CONTROLLING AND REPORTING (CONTD.)

Demonstrate understanding of the basic structure of the Balance Sheet and give examples of items which are commonly included in it.

A Balance Sheet is a clear statement of the assets of a company (what the business owns or is owed), its liabilities (what the business owes) and its capital at a particular moment in time (normally the end of an accounting period, e.g. the end of the financial year).

By studying the various parts of the Balance Sheet you can tell how sound the business is – especially if you compare one year with another or compare two businesses operating in a similar field, e.g. two high street banks.

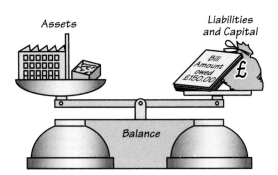

The balance sheet balances because in accounting all transactions are recorded twice – once on each side of the scale

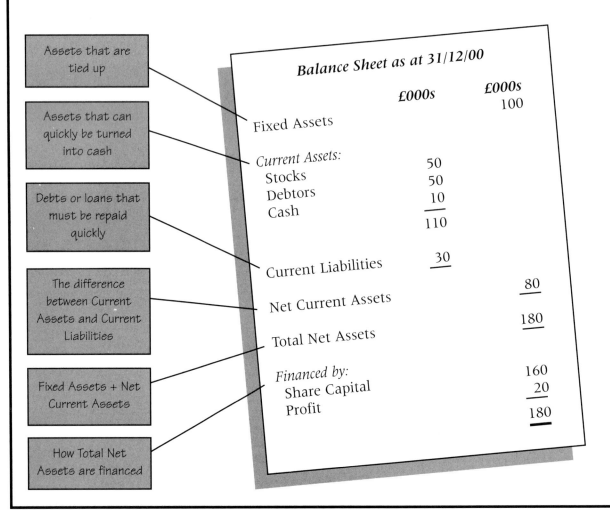

Assets that are tied up			
Assets that can quickly be turned into cash			
Debts or loans that must be repaid quickly			
The difference between Current Assets and Current Liabilities			
Fixed Assets + Net Current Assets			
How Total Net Assets are financed			

Balance Sheet as at 31/12/00

	£000s	£000s
Fixed Assets		100
Current Assets:		
Stocks	50	
Debtors	50	
Cash	10	
	110	
Current Liabilities	30	
Net Current Assets		80
Total Net Assets		180
Financed by:		
Share Capital		160
Profit		20
		180

3.4 PLANNING, CONTROLLING AND REPORTING (CONTD.)

Identify and calculate Working Capital.

Working Capital = Current Assets – Current Liabilities

Assets which the company can turn into cash in the short term are called **Current Assets.** They are ranked in order of liquidity:

1 Stocks *(least liquid)*
2 Debtors
3 Cash *(most liquid)*

Current Liabilities are debts that the company must pay within a year.

A sensible (prudent) **Working Capital Ratio** is **2 : 1**, i.e.:

Current Assets : Current Liabilities = 2 : 1

Businesses also use the **Quick Ratio** as follows:

Current Assets – Stock : Current
                                    Liabilities

A safe Quick Ratio is **1 : 1**.

Describe and explain the circular flow of Working Capital.

Working capital is used in a circular way.

Cash is used to buy **stocks** which are then sold on credit. Eventually the stocks are paid for – i.e. they are converted into cash. This cash is used to pay for more stocks.

The successful firm will turn stocks into sold goods which are quickly paid for.

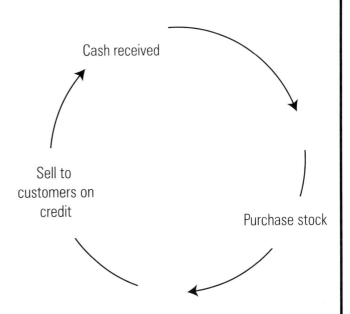

SHOW THAT YOU KNOW IT!

1   Define **marketing**.

2   Describe **four** ways in which a business can find out information about markets for its products.

3   Why are **piloting** and **sampling** important in field research?

4   Explain two ways of **segmenting** markets that would be suitable for a manufacturer of jeans.

5   What is meant by the **product life cycle**? When are the best times to advertise during the product life cycle of a family car?

6   What is the difference between **market orientation** and **product orientation**?

7   Explain the difference between **job** and **batch** production. Explain which method would be most suitable for organising production in a small bakery.

8   What is **process** production?

9   Why is **continuous flow production** widely used in modern mass production? Show how this method might be used in a particular industry.

10 What are **fixed** and **variable costs of production**? Give examples of these types of cost in a small taxi business.

11 What are (a) **direct costs** and (b) **indirect costs**? Why is it important to apportion indirect costs to particular products?

12 If a business has fixed costs of £10,000, sells its products for £10 a unit, and buys in the product for £8 per unit, what will be its **break-even point**?

13 What is meant by the **break-even point (BEP)**?

14 Define **economies of scale**. List and explain five major types of economy of scale that a large hotel might benefit from.

15 What are the benefits to business of operating on a **small scale**? Explain why a particular business can benefit from operating on a small scale.

16 What are **external** economies of scale? Give **two** examples.

17 What are the ingredients of the **marketing mix**?

18 Describe an appropriate marketing mix for a small fashion shop selling designer labels.

19 Explain **three price strategies** that might be appropriate for a small book publishing firm that has recently entered the market for specialist sports autobiographies.

20 What is **cash flow forecasting** and why is it important?

21 Define **profit** and explain why it is important to the business person.

22 A. Trader makes £60,000 worth of sales in 2001. Her opening stock was £5,000 and during the year she purchased £50,000 worth of stock. Her closing stock was £6,000. Set out her **trading accounts** and show her **Gross Profit**.

23 At the end of a year a business has fixed assets of £200,000, stocks worth £80,000, debtors of £60,000, cash of £20,000, and current liabilities of £100,000. What is its **Working Capital Ratio**?

24 What is a prudent **Working Capital Ratio**?

25 Draw a **diagram** to show the circular flow of Working Capital.

4.1 HUMAN NEEDS AND REWARDS

Explain the role of work in satisfying human needs.

People don't just work for money – they also work to fulfil their needs.

Abraham Maslow identified a **Hierarchy of Needs**:

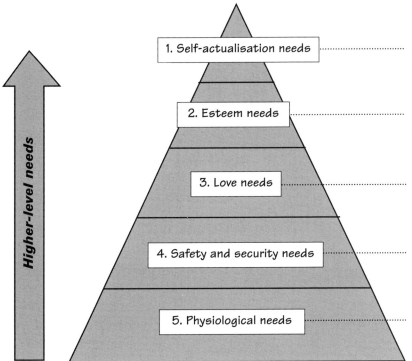

Higher-level needs

1. Self-actualisation needs
2. Esteem needs
3. Love needs
4. Safety and security needs
5. Physiological needs

How needs can be met in the workplace:

By encouraging employees to make decisions and to be creative

Through use of motivating job titles, and by recognising and rewarding effort and ability

By encouraging employees to work in a group or team

By maintaining high health and safety standards, and by providing adequate pension and sick pay

By paying employees enough for basic food, shelter and clothing

Human Resource Management means looking after people as if they are special in the workplace – finding out what their needs are and helping them to develop.

Frederick Herzberg believed that in order to motivate people, it is necessary to focus on creating 'satisfiers' in working relationships. Just creating 'dissatisfiers', i.e. punishing them for their mistakes or shortcomings, does not motivate people.

Dissatisfiers

◆ Having pay deducted or 'docked'
◆ Being punished for sloppy work

Satisfiers

◆ Being able to make your own decisions
◆ Taking on new work responsibilities
◆ Being part of a self-managing team

Punishment for poor work is a 'dissatisfier'

4.1 HUMAN NEEDS AND REWARDS (CONTD.)

Differentiate between types of work.

The occupational skills that workers need vary according to the type of work they do:

Unskilled work	Semi-skilled work	Skilled work
No training required, e.g., fruit or potato picker, programme-seller at football match, kitchen porter or washer-up	Some training required, e.g. general worker in supermarket, hospital porter	Extensive training required, e.g. airline pilot, brain surgeon, machinist in textile factory

Occupational skills are acquired by on-the-job and off-the-job training.

Explain different payment systems.

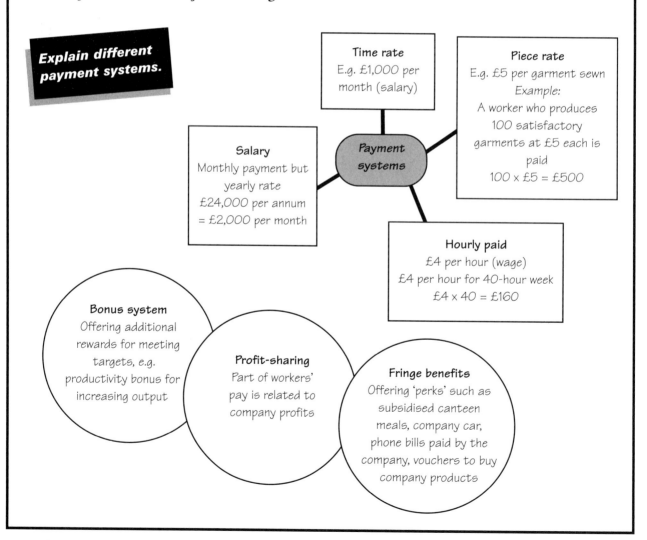

Time rate
E.g. £1,000 per month (salary)

Piece rate
E.g. £5 per garment sewn
Example:
A worker who produces 100 satisfactory garments at £5 each is paid
100 x £5 = £500

Salary
Monthly payment but yearly rate
£24,000 per annum
= £2,000 per month

Payment systems

Hourly paid
£4 per hour (wage)
£4 per hour for 40-hour week
£4 x 40 = £160

Bonus system
Offering additional rewards for meeting targets, e.g. productivity bonus for increasing output

Profit-sharing
Part of workers' pay is related to company profits

Fringe benefits
Offering 'perks' such as subsidised canteen meals, company car, phone bills paid by the company, vouchers to buy company products

4.1 HUMAN NEEDS AND REWARDS (CONTD.)

Evaluate the merits of different pay systems in different situations.

Payment system	Advantages	Disadvantages
Piece rates	◆ Encourages productivity ◆ Workers have an incentive to work for themselves	◆ May lead to accidents, waste and quality defects
Time rates	◆ Work is not spoilt by rushing ◆ Less stressful – employees feel valued	◆ No incentive to work quickly, ◆ May lead to low productivity
Bonus system	◆ Encourages people to work hard to meet targets ◆ Rewards those who work hardest	◆ Demotivating if targets are not met
Profit-sharing	◆ Employees identify with objectives of company ◆ Employee contributions are recognised	◆ Rewards those who may not have contributed to improvements
Fringe benefits	◆ Cheap to company, e.g. sale of company products at a discount can often be counted against tax	◆ Employees may abuse the system

Interpret and make calculations from pay slips.

Tax code shows how much income is tax-free

Pay advice	Name	Ref. no.	30 Dec. 2000
Toy Company PLC	John Brown	272687 2017 Code 0450H	Your net pay has been credited to your bank account

Basic Pay/ Additions		Deductions		Net Pay
Basic pay	1000.00	Nat. Insurance	210.00	
Overtime	200.00	Pension	70.00	
		Union	10.00	
Gross pay	**1200.00**	**Deductions**	**290.00**	**Net pay 910.00**

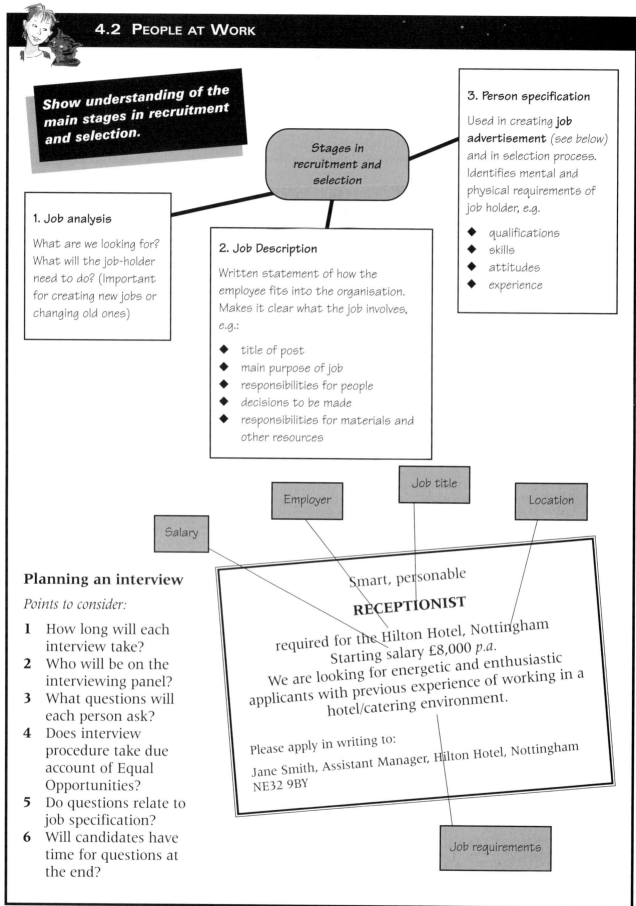

4.2 PEOPLE AT WORK

Show understanding of the main stages in recruitment and selection.

Stages in recruitment and selection

1. Job analysis

What are we looking for? What will the job-holder need to do? (Important for creating new jobs or changing old ones)

2. Job Description

Written statement of how the employee fits into the organisation. Makes it clear what the job involves, e.g.:

◆ title of post
◆ main purpose of job
◆ responsibilities for people
◆ decisions to be made
◆ responsibilities for materials and other resources

3. Person specification

Used in creating **job advertisement** (*see below*) and in selection process. Identifies mental and physical requirements of job holder, e.g.

◆ qualifications
◆ skills
◆ attitudes
◆ experience

Planning an interview

Points to consider:

1 How long will each interview take?
2 Who will be on the interviewing panel?
3 What questions will each person ask?
4 Does interview procedure take due account of Equal Opportunities?
5 Do questions relate to job specification?
6 Will candidates have time for questions at the end?

Salary

Employer

Job title

Location

Smart, personable

RECEPTIONIST

required for the Hilton Hotel, Nottingham
Starting salary £8,000 *p.a.*
We are looking for energetic and enthusiastic applicants with previous experience of working in a hotel/catering environment.

Please apply in writing to:

Jane Smith, Assistant Manager, Hilton Hotel, Nottingham NE32 9BY

Job requirements

4.2 PEOPLE AT WORK (CONTD.)

Describe and explain the importance of induction, training and development, and the relative advantages and drawbacks of internal and external training.

Training is the process of helping individuals to do their jobs better – i.e. to close the 'training gap'.

Career development
- Ongoing process
- 'Moving onwards and upwards'
- Career progression
- Becoming more knowledgeable and skilled
- Taking on more responsibilities

Induction
- 'Learning the ropes'
- Getting to know other workers
- Finding out about Health and Safety, legal requirements, etc.
- Finding out about the organisation

Aspects of training

Skills development
- Learning new skills
- Improving old skills
- Retraining for new work
- Keeping up with changes in the workplace or industry

Training then and now

Left and below: in the past, many apprentices learned 'on the job' or on day release at the local technical college

Above: a modern appraisal interview

4.2 PEOPLE AT WORK (CONTD.)

Understand the importance of continued training.

Training is not a 'one-off' experience. It is a way of continually improving workforce performance through a process of lifelong learning.

Type of training	Advantages	Disadvantages
Internal	◆ Cheaper to run ◆ Can be directly related to company needs ◆ Enables people inside a company to develop themselves by training others	◆ Brings nothing new into the company ◆ Doesn't challenge existing ways of doing things
External	◆ Brings in outside experts and new ideas ◆ Can draw on specialist training facilities that may not exist within company	◆ Can be very expensive and wasteful if not related directly to company needs

SHOW THAT YOU KNOW IT!

1 What are the **five** stages in **Maslow's Hierarchy of Needs**?

2 How can love needs, esteem needs and self-actualisation needs be met in the workplace?

3 Give examples of Herzberg's **satisfiers**. Why are they more likely to motivate employees than **dissatisfiers**?

4 Give an example of a **skilled**, a **semi-skilled** and an **unskilled** job.

5 How does an employee become **skilled**?

6 What is the difference between **piece** and **time rates**? Describe a situation where time rate may be better than piece rate, and another in which piece rate may be more suitable than time rate.

7 How is **profit-sharing** likely to motivate employees?

8 What is the purpose of giving **commission** to sales people?

9 List **four fringe benefits**.

10 Why might a company producing electrical components run a **bonus system** during some periods of the year?

11 What compulsory **deductions** are taken from a typical pay packet? List **three** possible voluntary deductions.

12 Why might **job analysis** be important in creating a new job?

13 What is a **job description**? What would it typically include?

14 How might a job description help a **new employee** at work?

15 Set out a **job advertisement** showing **six** key features.

16 List and explain **six** important stages in planning a **job interview**.

17 What is a **person specification**? What might it be used for?

18 What is **internal training**? What are the advantages of internal training?

19 What is **external training**? What are the advantages of external training?

20 Is training a **cost** or a **benefit** to a company?

21 What is **induction** and what might be included in an induction programme?

22 What is **career development**? Who is it important to?

23 When does training take place?

24 What is the **training gap**? Illustrate it.

25 Why do employees need **ongoing** skills training?

5.1 REASONS FOR REGULATING BUSINESS ACTIVITY

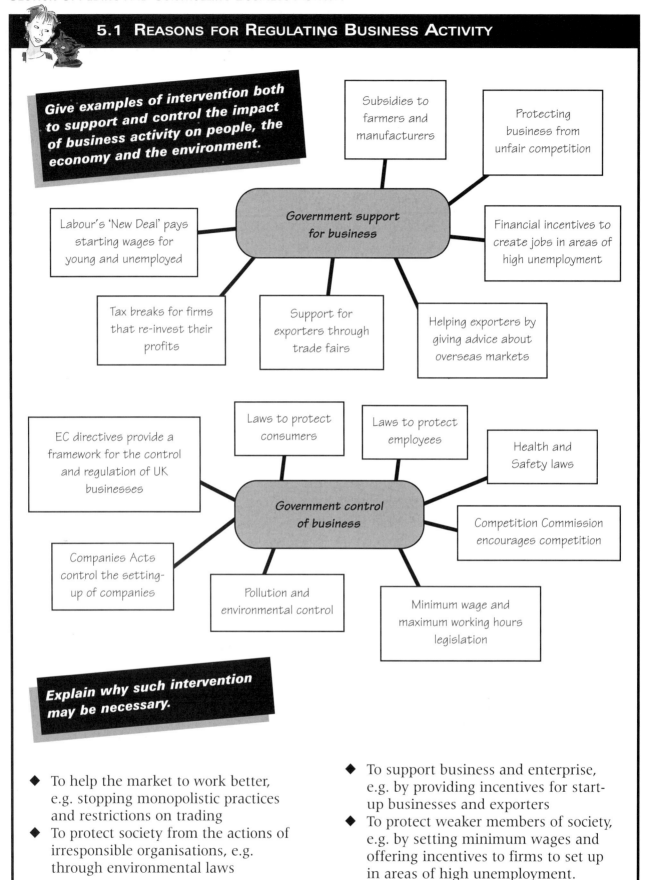

Give examples of intervention both to support and control the impact of business activity on people, the economy and the environment.

Subsidies to farmers and manufacturers

Protecting business from unfair competition

Labour's 'New Deal' pays starting wages for young and unemployed

Government support for business

Financial incentives to create jobs in areas of high unemployment

Tax breaks for firms that re-invest their profits

Support for exporters through trade fairs

Helping exporters by giving advice about overseas markets

EC directives provide a framework for the control and regulation of UK businesses

Laws to protect consumers

Laws to protect employees

Health and Safety laws

Government control of business

Competition Commission encourages competition

Companies Acts control the setting-up of companies

Pollution and environmental control

Minimum wage and maximum working hours legislation

Explain why such intervention may be necessary.

◆ To help the market to work better, e.g. stopping monopolistic practices and restrictions on trading
◆ To protect society from the actions of irresponsible organisations, e.g. through environmental laws

◆ To support business and enterprise, e.g. by providing incentives for start-up businesses and exporters
◆ To protect weaker members of society, e.g. by setting minimum wages and offering incentives to firms to set up in areas of high unemployment.

5.1 REASONS FOR REGULATING BUSINESS ACTIVITY (CONTD.)

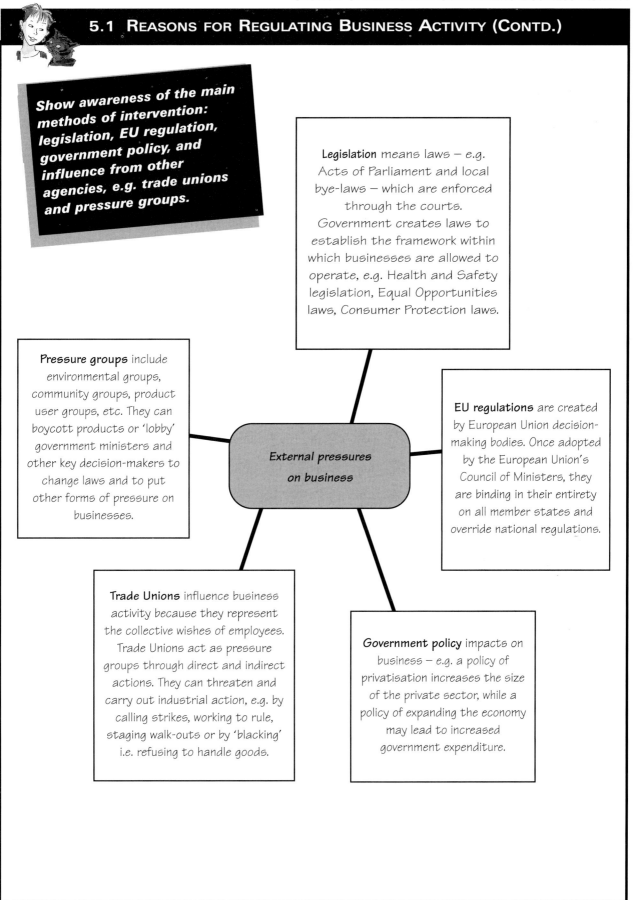

Show awareness of the main methods of intervention: legislation, EU regulation, government policy, and influence from other agencies, e.g. trade unions and pressure groups.

Legislation means laws – e.g. Acts of Parliament and local bye-laws – which are enforced through the courts. Government creates laws to establish the framework within which businesses are allowed to operate, e.g. Health and Safety legislation, Equal Opportunities laws, Consumer Protection laws.

Pressure groups include environmental groups, community groups, product user groups, etc. They can boycott products or 'lobby' government ministers and other key decision-makers to change laws and to put other forms of pressure on businesses.

External pressures on business

EU regulations are created by European Union decision-making bodies. Once adopted by the European Union's Council of Ministers, they are binding in their entirety on all member states and override national regulations.

Trade Unions influence business activity because they represent the collective wishes of employees. Trade Unions act as pressure groups through direct and indirect actions. They can threaten and carry out industrial action, e.g. by calling strikes, working to rule, staging walk-outs or by 'blacking' i.e. refusing to handle goods.

Government policy impacts on business – e.g. a policy of privatisation increases the size of the private sector, while a policy of expanding the economy may lead to increased government expenditure.

5.2 INFLUENCES ON BUSINESS ACTIVITY

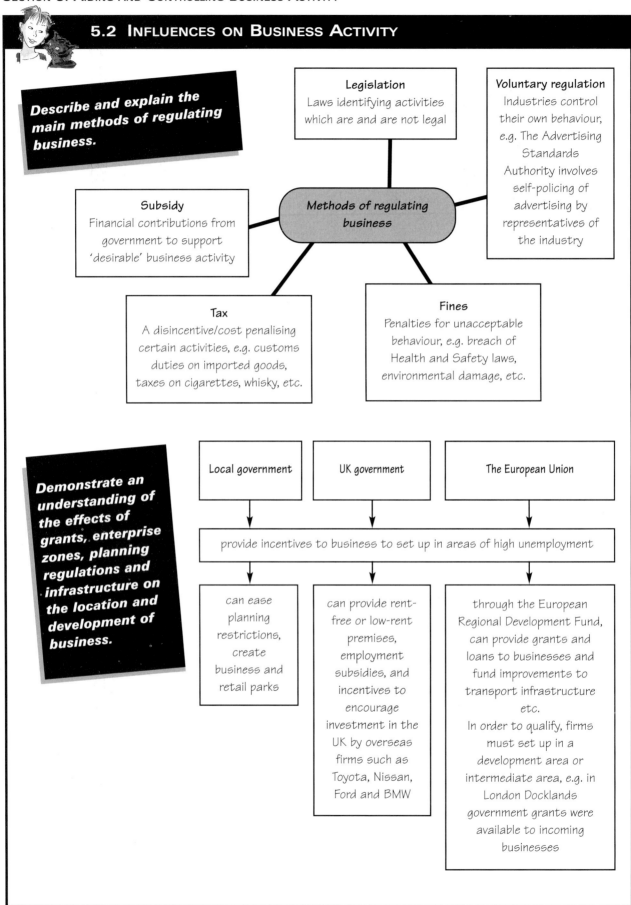

Describe and explain the main methods of regulating business.

Legislation
Laws identifying activities which are and are not legal

Voluntary regulation
Industries control their own behaviour, e.g. The Advertising Standards Authority involves self-policing of advertising by representatives of the industry

Subsidy
Financial contributions from government to support 'desirable' business activity

Methods of regulating business

Tax
A disincentive/cost penalising certain activities, e.g. customs duties on imported goods, taxes on cigarettes, whisky, etc.

Fines
Penalties for unacceptable behaviour, e.g. breach of Health and Safety laws, environmental damage, etc.

Demonstrate an understanding of the effects of grants, enterprise zones, planning regulations and infrastructure on the location and development of business.

Local government	UK government	The European Union

provide incentives to business to set up in areas of high unemployment

| can ease planning restrictions, create business and retail parks | can provide rent-free or low-rent premises, employment subsidies, and incentives to encourage investment in the UK by overseas firms such as Toyota, Nissan, Ford and BMW | through the European Regional Development Fund, can provide grants and loans to businesses and fund improvements to transport infrastructure etc. In order to qualify, firms must set up in a development area or intermediate area, e.g. in London Docklands government grants were available to incoming businesses |

5.2 INFLUENCES ON BUSINESS ACTIVITY (CONTD.)

Describe the work of trade unions, the main types of industrial action and the main methods of resolving conflict.

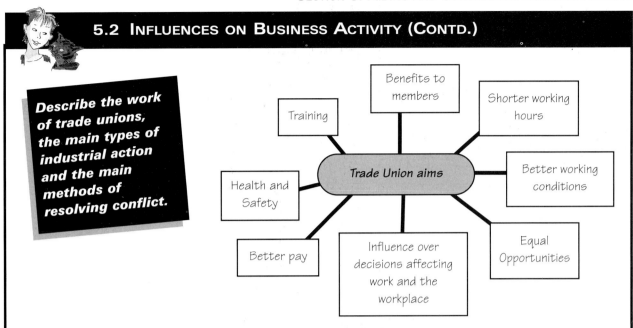

Trade Union aims

- Benefits to members
- Training
- Shorter working hours
- Health and Safety
- Better working conditions
- Better pay
- Influence over decisions affecting work and the workplace
- Equal Opportunities

Trade unions are formed, financed and run by their members. In law they must be independent of their employer. A union will have full-time officials, usually at a regional level. Within the trade union organisation, members are represented by **shop stewards**.

Unofficial action occurs when union members take action which is not approved by the union executive.

Types of union action include:

- ◆ **Strike**: workers withdraw their labour.
- ◆ **Work-to-rule**: workers stick strictly to the rulebook in a pedantic way to reduce productivity and output
- ◆ **Ban on overtime**: members refuse to work outside normal working hours
- ◆ **Withdrawal of goodwill**: workers stop doing things which they usually co-operate with management in doing

Resolving industrial disputes

Ways of resolving conflict include:

- ◆ Setting up **co-determination groups** between managers and workers to make joint decisions

- ◆ Referring disputes to the **Advisory, Conciliation and Arbitration Service** (ACAS). ACAS has Codes of Practice which provide a quick way of resolving disputes.
- ◆ **Conciliation** involves helping to bring the two sides to an agreement.
- ◆ **Arbitration** means making a decision which the two parties in a dispute agree to abide by.

"I wonder if I should join a trade union…"

"If you did, I wouldn't let you work for me!"

5.2 INFLUENCES ON BUSINESS ACTIVITY (CONTD.)

Demonstrate an understanding of the importance of Health and Safety requirements and how they affect business.

"There's far too much fuss about Health and Safety these days – if employees can't be bothered to take commonsense safety precautions, that's their funeral!"

Is Ron Right?

Who is responsible for Health and Safety?

◆ **Employers:** all firms with more than five workers must have a safety policy.

◆ **Employees:** all employees must take responsibility for their own safety and the safety of those they work with. They must work in a safe way and report any accidents.

The **Health and Safety at Work Act** declares that 'the employer has a duty to ensure the health, safety and welfare at work of all employees' as far as is reasonably practical.

Employers and employees must also be aware of:

◆ Reporting of Injuries, Diseases and Dangerous Occurrences Regulations (RIDDOR)
◆ Control of Substances Hazardous to Health (COSHH)
◆ Noise at Work Regulations – to protect employees against risk of hearing damage.

In spite of government regulations, unsafe practices still exist in many workplaces

5.2 INFLUENCES ON BUSINESS ACTIVITY (CONTD.)

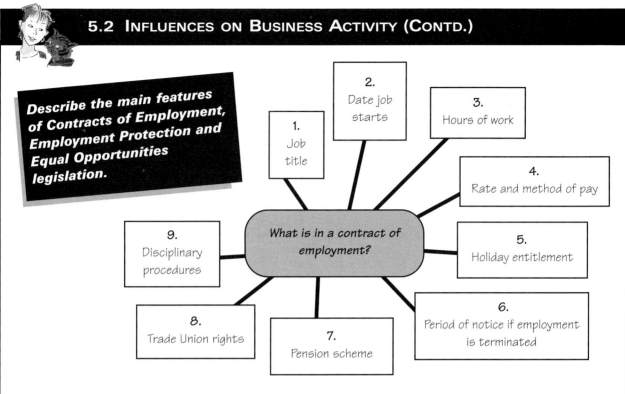

Describe the main features of Contracts of Employment, Employment Protection and Equal Opportunities legislation.

What is in a contract of employment?

1. Job title
2. Date job starts
3. Hours of work
4. Rate and method of pay
5. Holiday entitlement
6. Period of notice if employment is terminated
7. Pension scheme
8. Trade Union rights
9. Disciplinary procedures

A new employee must be given a written contract within 13 weeks. But a contract exists in law from the moment when the employer offers the job and the employee accepts.

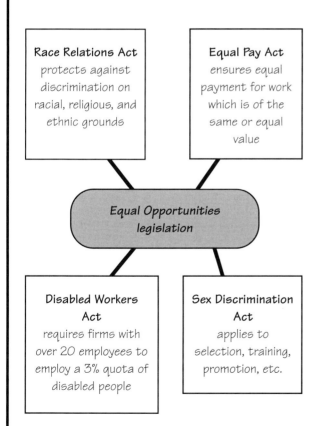

Race Relations Act protects against discrimination on racial, religious, and ethnic grounds

Equal Pay Act ensures equal payment for work which is of the same or equal value

Equal Opportunities legislation

Disabled Workers Act requires firms with over 20 employees to employ a 3% quota of disabled people

Sex Discrimination Act applies to selection, training, promotion, etc.

The employee is protected in law against **unfair dismissal**. Grounds for claiming unfair dismissal include:

◆ harassment at work
◆ union membership
◆ racial discrimination
◆ pregnancy

Fair dismissal may be for offences such as harrassing others, wilful destruction of company property and continuous bad timekeeping.

The Acts shown on the left apply to both **direct discrimination** and **indirect discrimination** (i.e. conditions which particular groups are less likely to be able to comply with, e.g. requirement that employees must wear short skirts or not have long hair).

5.2 INFLUENCES ON BUSINESS ACTIVITY (CONTD.)

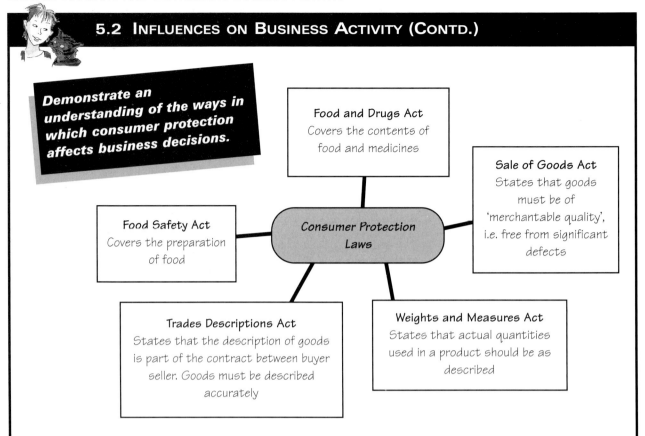

Demonstrate an understanding of the ways in which consumer protection affects business decisions.

Food and Drugs Act
Covers the contents of food and medicines

Sale of Goods Act
States that goods must be of 'merchantable quality', i.e. free from significant defects

Food Safety Act
Covers the preparation of food

Consumer Protection Laws

Trades Descriptions Act
States that the description of goods is part of the contract between buyer seller. Goods must be described accurately

Weights and Measures Act
States that actual quantities used in a product should be as described

Consumers are protected by laws and voluntary codes of practice.

Businesses that fail to look after consumers can be fined by the courts and will certainly lose sales as a result of bad publicity.

The local council's **Trading Standards Department** investigates firms that give false or misleading descriptions of their products or inaccurate information about quantities, weights and measures, etc. The local **Environmental Health Department** investigates restaurants, food shops, etc., to examine standards of hygiene and food safety.

SHOW THAT YOU KNOW IT!

1 Give **five** examples of government actions which support business activity.

2 How does government **competition policy** benefit business?

3 List **six** ways in which the government **controls** business activity. Explain one of these controls.

4 Why is government **intervention** in the economy necessary?

5 What is an **EU regulation** and what status does it have in the UK?

6 Explain how **one** government policy impacts on business.

7 Describe and explain how government regulation and activity might affect (**a**) a farmer, and (**b**) a small shopkeeper.

8 How does government encourage business to move to areas of high unemployment?

9 Describe **two** aims that a trade union might have in a car-manufacturing plant.

10 What actions would you suggest that a trade union takes if it is unable to gain what it considers to be a fair wage increase in pay bargaining with management?

11 What is the role of **ACAS** in resolving industrial disputes?

12 Who is responsible for **Health and Safety** in the workplace?

13 What are **RIDDOR** and **COSHH**?

14 When does a **contract of employment** become binding in law? List **six** features that would be included in a contract of employment.

15 What are the **four** key areas of **Equal Opportunities** legislation?

16 What is covered by the **Disabled Workers Act**?

17 What is (**a**) **direct** and (**b**) **indirect** discrimination?

18 Give an **example** of indirect discrimination.

19 What is covered by the **Race Relations Act**?

20 Explain **two** ways in which an employee may claim that they have been **unfairly dismissed**.

21 What is the difference between a **law** and a **voluntary code of practice**?

22 What is covered by (**a**) the **Sale of Goods Act**, and (**b**) the **Trades Descriptions Act**?

23 What is the **Food Safety Act** concerned with?

24 What is the function of the **Trading Standards Department**?

25 What is the function of the **Environmental Health Department**?

Test Yourself in Exam Conditions

The main types of examination used at GCSE are:

1 An extended case study with several weeks pre-reading time
2 A case study which you only see in the exam room, which is broken up into a number of segments.

Both types of exam set out to test the same range of objectives. Test yourself using the two papers which are provided below.

Test Paper 1: Extended Case Study

A Corporate Gift

Time: 1 hour and 30 minutes. (You can spend as much time as you want reading through and making notes on the case before you start writing)

Peter Millward has been interested in designing and making clocks from an early age. As a teenager he enjoyed making and painting miniature models, and when he was 14, in his technology work at school, he produced his first clock. His school also found him a three-week work experience placement at a local firm which specialised in repairing and restoring old clocks. For Peter it was like a dream come true to be in the workshop using the tools and equipment of a skilled worker.

Peter spent all his weekends and holidays picking up 'on-the-job' experience and at sixteen he was taken on as an apprentice by the firm he had attended on work experience. However, he realised that in order to progress, he also needed further qualifications. So during his apprenticeship he also studied in his own time and took A-levels at college. He then left his job and went on to the Central School of Art and Design, where he specialised in various aspects of design.

After leaving college, Peter worked for a short period for a design studio. However, much of his time was taken up with routine tasks and he rarely saw a job through from beginning to end. So he decided to set up his own business in the form of a private company. His father and uncle bought shares in the company, as did a friend of the family. Peter decided the company should trade under the name Corporoclocks.

The idea for **Corporoclocks** came from Peter's experiences of working at the studio. He was shown a sample of some clocks which the studio was designing for a local company to use as:

a) long-service awards
b) promotional items and free gifts to promote the company image.

Peter was sure that with his experience, he could create a much better design and also improve the quality of the clocks.

The market at the time was mainly being supplied by a few firms producing a range of items sold from glossy catalogues. Where clocks were offered they were generally of poor quality and were not seen as particularly unique or prestigious corporate items. Nobody specialised in this particular field of corporate gift. Peter felt that he had identified a niche market he could supply. He had always wanted to work and earn money for himself rather than for others, and here was the perfect chance to do it.

Continued on page 68

A Corporate Gift (Contd.)

Peter knew that the products he could produce would be clearly differentiated from any others on the market and could be used as long-service gifts or as promotional items for privileged customers.

The Business Plan

Peter's first task was to draw up a business plan and then approach a bank for help in the form of a £5,000 loan. Peter's plan included details of his ideas, evidence of the research he had undertaken and his financial proposals. For example, he had estimated that his **fixed costs** in his first year of trading, which included all setting-up costs and interest payments, would be £8,000. Each clock would sell, on average, for £25 and the **variable costs** involved in manufacture would include:

£4 direct labour per unit
£1 direct materials per unit
£1 other variable costs

With the machinery and tools he intended to purchase, Peter estimated that he could produce about 1,200 clocks in his first year of trading. Peter's proposals also took into account the need for secretarial help and expenditure on office technology.

Peter chose some small premises just outside London, so that he could remain close to where the majority of his customers were based. As he would occasionally have to be off the premises to sell his ideas and products, he did not want to have to keep making long journey which would increase his costs and also take up considerable time – time when he could be working on his clocks.

Peter soon managed to identify and create a broad customer base which included many household names. He found that the best way of making contact with a prospective client was to ring up a company and ask for the name of the person responsible for buying business gifts. The next stage involved writing to that person in order to secure an appointment. He always attached a mailshot with his letter.

Peter's priority is to make sure that his clocks are precision-made and that he meets orders on time. Though his business is quickly going from strength to strength, he is wary about expanding too quickly as he wants to build up and develop relationships with existing clients.

Questions

1 Explain **two advantages** to Peter of setting up his business close to London.
(4 marks)

2 Explain **one disadvantage** to Peter of setting up his business close to London.
(2 marks)

3 What was the **opportunity cost** to Peter of setting up in business?
(4 marks)

4 What **benefits** would Peter have gained from setting up the business as a **private company** rather than as a sole trader?
(6 marks)

5 What is **niche marketing**?
(3 marks)

6 From the case, describe **two** elements of the **marketing mix** for the product that Corporoclocks is developing.
(6 marks)

7   Corporoclocks borrowed money by means of a bank loan. Explain the advantages of **two** other methods of **external finance** that Peter could have used.

(8 marks)

8   How might Corporoclocks be affected by a change in **interest rates**?

(6 marks)

9   a) Corporoclocks is going to advertise for part-time secretarial help for 10 hours a week at £4.50 per hour. Design an **advert** which Peter could use in the local press.

(8 marks)

    b) Create a **job description** for the part-time post.

(8 marks)

    c) Explain how Peter could plan an **interview** for the post.

(8 marks)

10 a) Calculate Corporoclocks' **break-even point**.

(6 marks)

    b) How much **profit** will Peter make if he manages to sell 1,200 clocks?

(2 marks)

    c) Why will **cash flow forecasting** be important to Corporoclocks?

(6 marks)

11 Show how Corporoclocks could find out about the **market** for its clocks.

(6 marks)

12 How might Corporoclocks **segment** its market?

(6 marks)

13 What are the benefits to Corporoclocks of operating on a **small scale**?

(5 marks)

14 Describe **three** items which are likely to appear in the **assets** side of the balance sheet for Corporoclocks.

(6 marks)

Test Paper 2: Segmented Case Study

Super Sandwiches

Time: 2 hours

Super Sandwiches is a small shop selling sandwiches in the business district of a medium-sized town in the Midlands. The table below show the fixed, variable and total costs that Super Sandwiches Ltd has calculated it would have to pay each day at different levels of output (i.e. number of sandwiches produced for sale).

Super Sandwiches Ltd: Costs and Revenue per day				
Output per day	Fixed cost £	Variable cost £	Total cost £	Total revenue £
200	300	50	350	200
300	300	75	375	300
400	300	100	400	400
500	300	125	425	500
600	300	150	450	600

Questions

1 a) Using the data contained in the table, plot a **break-even chart** based on the graph below.

(6 marks)

Revenues and costs (£)

Output per week

b) How many sandwiches did Super Sandwiches Ltd need to sell per day in order to break even?

(2 marks)

2 The **costs** that Super Sandwiches Ltd have to pay include:

labour
rent of the premises
cost of bread
cost of fillings
cost of electricity
business rates

a) Which of the above costs are **fixed costs**?

(2 marks)

b) Which of the above costs are **variable costs**?

(2 marks)

3 Super Sandwiches produces sandwiches in batches at the start of each day. Why is **batch production** suitable for sandwich production?

(4 marks)

4 Super Sandwiches was originally set up by Jenny Broughton and her friend Sally Smith. However, they soon converted the business to a private company.

a) State **two** features of partnerships.

(2 marks)

b) What additional advantages would there be to converting the business to a **private limited company**?

(6 marks)

5 When Jenny and Sally originally set up the business they calculated that they needed to raise £40,000. The main things that they had to pay for were:

Downpayment on rent of shop
Cost of machinery and equipment
Cost of advertising
Cost of raw materials
Electricity costs
Wages

Choose **one** cost from the list above. State **two** possible ways of financing the cost. Give reasons why the methods of finance that you state are suitable:

a) First method of finance

(3 marks)

b) Second method of finance

(3 marks)

6 Explain how Super Sandwiches **adds value** in the process of production of sandwiches.

(4 marks)

7 a) Explain how the ingredients that Super Sandwiches uses will have originally been produced in the **primary sector** of the economy.

(4 marks)

b) Under which sector of the economy would you classify Super Sandwiches?

(1 mark)

8 Explain one possible **business objective** that Super Sandwiches might have.

(2 marks)

9 Super Sandwiches are thinking about **franchising** their business idea in different parts of the UK. How might Super Sandwiches benefit from franchising out their idea?

(6 marks)

10 How might people taking out a Super Sandwiches franchise benefit from taking out a franchise rather than setting up independently on their own?

(8 marks)

11 Describe **three** ways in which the **government** influences the activities of Super Sandwiches.

(6 marks)

12 Super Sandwiches wishes to employ an experienced accountant to look after the business accounts. Jenny and Sally have created the following advertisement:

Super Sandwiches requires experienced

Part-time Accountant

Contact: Super Sandwiches,
5 High Street Midtown, MD2 6WN

Do you think that the advertisement will help the business to appoint the right person they need? Give reasons for your answer.

(5 marks)

13 Super Sandwiches want to create a **job description** for the new part-time accountant. What sorts of details should be included in it?

(6 marks)

14 Super Sandwiches is also hoping to appoint a number of part-time employees to work in their premises at peak times. Why might they need to design an **induction programme** for their new employees?

(6 marks)

15 Why might Super Sandwiches need to design different types of sandwiches to appeal to different **segments** of their market?

(6 marks)

16 Design a **marketing strategy** which might be suitable to enable Super Sandwiches to attract a particular group of customers.

(12 marks)

17 How might a business like Super Sandwiches benefit from **government funding**?

(4 marks)

Answers

Section 1: The External Environment of the Business

Show That You Know It! page 19

1. Economic activities are the processes that add value to goods – e.g. in the case of Coca-Cola, mixing and blending ingredients, marketing, packaging and distribution all add value to the final product.

2. **Adding value** to products makes them more desirable to the final consumer – each step gives them a bit more of what they want.

3. Goods are **scarce** because there aren't enough of them to meet everyone's needs and desires. They are scarce relative to requirements.

4. The **opportunity cost** of revising GCSE Business Studies is the next-best alternative sacrificed, e.g. a visit to the cinema or a game of football in the park.

5. The **real cost** to a firm of investing in a new factory is the next-best thing it could have done with the investment capital, e.g. pay for a new distribution network, or award a pay rise to employees.

6. **Primary** occupations include oil driller, coal miner, farm labourer, fisherman. **Secondary** occupations include shoe-maker, construction worker, film maker, textile worker. **Tertiary** occupations include police officer, insurance clerk, bank manager, professional footballer, marketing director.

7. The **service sector** of the economy provides the largest share of employment. In a post-industrial society consumers attach most value to personal services, e.g. hairdressing, cosmetic treatment. Business services are also important, e.g. insurance, banking, transport, etc. Service-sector jobs are a lot more labour-intensive than secondary and primary-sector jobs, where it is often easier to use automated production processes.

8. Service-sector occupations usually involve some form of direct dealing with people – e.g. banking, insurance, hairdressing, counselling, etc. **Personal relationships** are particularly important. Customers tend to buy from service organisations that recognise their individual needs.

9. The **feminisation** of work means that more women are entering the labour force (nearly half of all jobs in the British economy are done by women). However, many of these jobs involve part-time and temporary work, where pay and conditions tend to be worse than full-time permanent jobs. Some women are earning more than before, but the benefits are not spread evenly among the workforce.

10. The major factor leading to rises in productivity has been the mechanisation and automation of work processes in recent years, often supported by use of **Information Technology**.

11. Areas that have seen industrial decline include large parts of Scotland, the North East, The North West, The West Midlands and the South West, as well as large parts of Wales. These areas tend to be on the edges of economic activity and have traditionally depended on heavy industries which have been in decline, e.g. steel, coal, shipbuilding, textiles and engineering.

12. There are 350 million people in the European Union. The UK joined in 1973.

13. The EU encourages greater competition because it provides a **Single Market** in which large European firms can compete with each other without any protective taxes and tariffs.

14. Many large businesses are in favour of a single currency (the Euro) because this would cut out the need (and the

cost) of changing money from one European currency to another. It would also add stability to the price of currencies over time.

15 The Four Freedoms are the movement of people, capital, goods and services.

16 Business objectives include:

◆ maximising **profits** (i.e. achieving the greatest possible difference between total revenues and costs),
◆ **survival** (keeping in business)
◆ **maximising sales** (selling as much as possible and outselling rivals)
◆ **growth** (expanding the size of the business).

17 **Profit** can be measured by Total Revenue – Total Cost; **market share** can be measured by the market share of a particular company divided by the market share of its nearest rival; **growth** can be measured in a number of ways including the growth in the size of turnover and the size of profits; **wealth creation** can be measured by factors such as returns to shareholders and returns to employees.

18 **Consumers** purchase goods and put pressure on producers to meet their requirements; **employees** contribute to production through their efforts in adding value; the **government** provides an infrastructure of services that supports business as well as regulating business activity to make sure that it is carried out fairly; **taxpayers** provide revenues to the government which enable it to support business; and the **community** puts pressure on business to behave in a socially desirable way.

19 The **public sector** of the economy is owned by the government while the **private sector** is owned by private individuals and institutions.

20 **Private-sector businesses** include sole traders, partners, private companies, public companies, franchises and co-operatives. Public-sector businesses include public corporations and municipal (local council) enterprises.

21 **Privatisation** is the transfer of a business from the public to the private sector. Industries that have recently been privatised include rail, coal, electricity, water, steel, and gas.

22 A **deficit budget** exists when the government spends more than it raises in taxes. The government may run a deficit budget in order to pump demand into the economy during a period of unemployment.

23 **Business size** can be measured by:

a) the number of employees in a company
b) the size of its turnover
c) the profit made by a company
d) the number of sites from which the company operates
e) the volume of its output.

24 At the end of the day, it is the consumer who buys the company's product or service – customers who are not satisfied can always buy from a rival producer.

25 Some businesses operate in a very competitive environment in which the actions of rivals need to be carefully watched. If a company is able to add more value to a product than its competitors, it may be able to tempt customers away from rivals.

Section 2: Business Structure and Organisation

Show That You Know It! page 30

1 In law, a company is a **legal entity** that is separate from the people who own it (shareholders). However, in sole trader and partner businesses the law recognises the owner(s) as having a legal standing.

2 It might be advantageous to set up a small shop as a sole trader rather than a partnership because the owner(s) could then make decisions

independently, take all the profits and rely on their own judgement rather than having to consult others.

3   A private company has **limited liability**; is owned by **shareholders**, does not sell **shares** to the general public; has to be **registered** with the registrar of companies; has at least two shareholders; will often take the form of a **family business** (although some private companies such as Mars are much larger).

4   **Public Limited Companies (PLCs)** include Shell and BP, Barclays, Heinz and Cadbury Schweppes. PLCs are able to raise more capital than private companies; are able to sell shares on the Stock Exchange, and generally benefit more from economies of scale than private companies.

5   The **BBC** is a **public corporation** set up by Royal Charter, but some public corporations are set up by Acts of Parliament. The chairperson of a public corporation is chosen by a government minister. The chair and board of a public corporation are responsible for managing the corporation on a day-to-day basis although the government and parliament can intervene in long-term strategic decision-making.

6   Public corporations are accountable to consumers through a **consumers' council**, as well as being accountable to a parliamentary committee. Questions about the running of a public corporation can be asked in the Houses of Parliament.

7   **Retail co-operatives** are set up to benefit shoppers, and profits are usually shared among consumers in proportion to their purchases. Consumers are able to become members of the co-operative by buying a £1 share and can attend meetings to discuss policy. Co-operatives take a stance on social and ethical issues as well as running on commercial lines.

8   **Partners** have control over the running of a partnership. The main sources of finance are partners' capital, bank loans and other funds such as mortgages and credit. Profits are distributed according to an agreement set out in a **Deed of Partnership**.

9   The most common objectives of companies include making a profit, becoming the market leader, and seeking business growth.

10   The **sources of finance** for a sole trader are largely owners' capital, loans, mortgages and credit. Sources of finance for a Plc include shares, debentures, loans, mortgages, and credit arrangements.

11   A **public corporation** or **charity** organisation would make a surplus rather than a profit.

12   The **government** sets out to control the general level of business activity in the economy. It taxes anti-social behaviour such as smoking; it provides transport services to remote or outlying areas; it taxes business, and it generally provides the rules according to which businesses are able to carry it out their activities.

13   Coca-Cola runs a **franchise** of its bottling operations; Benetton franchises a number of retail outlets. Reasons for taking out a franchise are that franchisees can trade under a well-known name; draw on the expertise and training facilities of the franchising company; run their business in conjunction with the franchising company, and work to a tried and tested business formula.

14   *See diagram, p.76.*

15   A **flat** organisation cuts out much of the problems associated with tall, vertical communications – i.e. the length of time required to make decisions and pass messages down a hierarchical organisation. Flatter organisations also empower employees lower down the organisation, particularly enabling them to communicate with customers.

16   Sole traders and partners usually raise

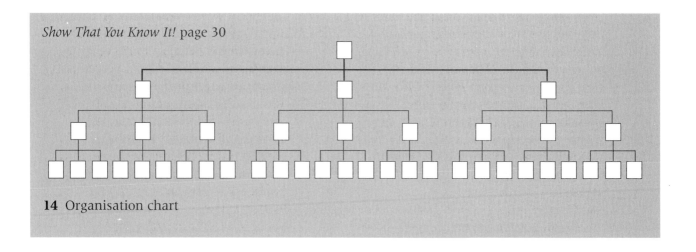

Show That You Know It! page 30

14 Organisation chart

their **starting capital** from their owners and also from bank loans.

17 A **Balance Sheet** is a snapshot showing the financial standing of a company at a particular moment in time. It sets out the company's capital, assets and liabilities.

18 A **cash flow forecast** makes it possible to predict likely future flows of cash in and out of the business and to forecast any temporary difficulties that might occur so that remedial action can be taken.

19 **Long-term finance** is required for the major capital projects of an organisation whereas **short-term finance** is required for meeting the cost of day-to-day activities.

20 The main sources of **internal** finance for private-sector organisations include owners' capital (including shareholders' capital) and profits.

21 **External** finance comes from trade credit, overdraft, bank loans, mortgages, hire purchase and leasing.

22 The main source of external finance for public-sector organisations are government grants and subsidies.

23 The type of finance raised depends on the nature of the risk involved, the length of time that the money is needed for, the type of project involved and the type of business.

24 The type of **project** influences the type of finance needed, e.g. for new buildings the finance will come from a mortgage; for a photocopier or vehicle, by hire purchase or leasing arrangement; goods can also be bought on trade credit, etc.

25 Overdrafts are often cheaper than loans because interest is only charged on the amount outstanding at a particular moment in time.

Section 3: Business Behaviour

Show That You Know It! page 50

1 **Marketing** is the process of anticipating, identifying and meeting customer requirements in order to make a profit.

2 Business can find out information about its markets by carrying out **market research** – i.e. by conducting questionnaires and surveys – or it can carry out qualitative research by setting up interview and testing panels using representative groups of consumers. Alternatively, it can examine information already available in the organisation itself – e.g. existing sales patterns. It can also look at how its competitors are responding to consumer requirements.

3 **Piloting** involves testing research on a small scale before carrying it out on a large scale. This saves a lot of money and effort at a later stage and enables methods of research to be refined.

Sampling involves carrying out market research with just one section of the total population who use or may use a product, in order to draw out wider generalisations. In this way research costs can be kept to a minimum.

4   A manufacturer of jeans could **segment** the market by **age** (because different age groups have different tastes and buying patterns). The market could also be segmented by **gender**, or according to **income**.

5   The **product life-cycle** is the series of stages that a product goes through from the time it is first thought of. The chief stages are launch, growth, maturity and eventual decline.

6   **Market orientation** is when an organisation's decisions are governed by what the consumer or customer wants, rather than by what the company *thinks* the customer should want. **Product orientation** is where the company tries to dictate to the consumer what sorts of products they should be buying, based on the company's expertise in producing that product.

7   **Job production** exists when an organisation specialises in individual one-off jobs of work, e.g. building a specialist cruise liner. **Batch production** exists when a firm produces batches of products, e.g. a batch of buns, before a batch of something else. Batch production is suitable for bakery work.

8   **Process production** occurs where the production cycle is broken down into a number of discrete processes – each of which is usually the responsibility of a team working with machinery allocated to that process. The process team will process the work and then pass it on for the next process to be carried out.

9   **Continuous flow production** is widely used because it can be carried out 24 hours a day, and for six or seven days a week. Once the line has been set up it does not require altering, allowing hundreds of thousands of identical (say) Mars bars to be produced over a period of months or years. Continuous flow production is common in food-processing plants – particularly those producing recipe dishes, biscuits and chocolate bars.

10 **Fixed costs** of production do not vary with the level of output. They have to be incurred in order to produce goods. **Variable costs** vary in proportion to the level of output. In a small taxi business, fixed costs might include the cost of renting the firm's central office and the cost of the fixed taxes, licences and fees that have to be paid to local government. Variable costs would include the cost of fuel used in the taxis – telephone charges, etc.

11 **Direct costs** are costs that can be directly related to the production of a particular item or product – for example, the labour that goes into producing a particular product. **Indirect costs** are those which cannot be so clearly associated with particular products – e.g. labour costs that are spread over a number of product lines – e.g. the lighting and heating costs in a factory.

12 Products are bought for £8 and sold for £10 – each individual product making £2 (assuming that the variable cost is the cost of buying-in the products for resale). Dividing the fixed cost, £10,000, by £2 gives a break-even point of 5,000 units of output.

13 The **break-even point** is the point at which the business is able to generate just enough revenue (from sales) to cover its total costs (fixed and variable costs).

14 **Economies of scale** are the advantages of producing on a large rather than a small scale. Economies of scale enable the firm to produce a larger output at a lower unit cost.

◆   A **technical economy of scale** that a large hotel might have is that it could have a much bigger swimming pool than a smaller hotel which might only cost a little more to clean and maintain.

◆ A **managerial economy** might be the employment of specialist kitchen and restaurant managers rather than general managers.

◆ A **marketing economy** would be that of being able to afford larger print-runs of promotional materials which would not be proportionately more expensive than smaller runs.

◆ A **risk-spreading economy** might be that of offering extra facilities that guests and outside customers could pay for, e.g. windsurfing, water-skiing, discos, etc.

◆ A **financial economy** might be that of being able to sell shares to shareholders at lower prices per share because of the scale of the share issue.

15 A **small-scale** business benefits by being able to offer a more personal service to customers; by operating in a niche market (e.g. left-handed golf clubs); by not having to employ large quantities of employees, and through not having to bear heavy overhead costs. Small businesses often serve larger businesses by providing specialist services to them, e.g. a large multinational company may well require specialist design and photographic services.

16 **External economies of scale** occur when part of an industry grows in such a way that individual firms are able to reduce their unit costs. Examples include the development of a motorway to an existing industrial area, lowering transport costs, and the development of feeder industries to a larger, more established industry.

17 The four main ingredients of the **marketing mix** are **Product, Price, Promotion, and Place**.

18 A shop selling designer labels would want to develop exclusive products, i.e. top designer names, which it could sell at a premium price to emphasise quality and uniqueness. It would need to promote its products through upmarket media, e.g. glossy magazines, and it would need to be in an upmarket location, e.g. a prime High Street spot.

19 Appropriate **pricing strategies** are:

a) **promotional** pricing, i.e. to set a price that would attract customers to the store. This might involve discount prices to start off with.

b) a **skimming** pricing strategy – i.e. starting with relatively high prices for exclusive books and then lowering the price to attract new, more downmarket segments of the overall market.

c) **destroyer** pricing – seeking to destroy the market of a rival by undercutting its prices.

20 **Cash flow** is concerned with setting out the likely inflow and outflow of cash over a projected period, in order to make sure that money coming in more than offsets money flowing out.

21 **Profit** is the excess of total revenue over total costs. The business person needs profit as a reward for the risk that they are taking as well as to provide them with a livelihood which is more than the opportunity cost of setting up in business.

22

Trading Account for A. Trader for the year ending 31st December		
	£	£
Sales	60,000	
Less Cost of Sales		
Opening Stock	5,000	
Add Purchases	60,000	
		65,000
Less Closing Stock	6,000	59,000
Gross Profit		1,000

23 Working Capital Ratio = Current Assets : Current Liabilities.
In this case, Current Assets consist of stocks, debtors and cash, i.e. £80,000 + £60,000 + £20,000 = £160,000 Current liabilities are £100,000.
Therefore the Working Capital Ratio is 16 : 10 which can be simplified to 8:5.

24 A prudent working capital ratio is 2:1.

25 See diagram on p.49.

Section 4: People in Business

Show That You Know It! page 57

1 Physiological needs, safety and security needs, love needs, esteem needs, and finally at the pinnacle, self-actualisation needs.

2 **Love needs** could be met in the workplace by getting people working together in team structures so they feel a sense of belonging. **Esteem needs** could be met by promoting people and giving them recognition through awards and job titles. **Self-actualisation** needs can be met by giving employees the opportunity to be creative and to put something of themselves into their work.

3 **Herzberg's satisfiers** include recognition of achievement, responsibilities and opportunities for promotion. All these factors encourage motivation.

4 A **skilled** job would include craft work in the creation of silverware or exclusive hairdressing. **Semi-skilled** work would include operating the tills at a supermarket. **Unskilled** work would include cleaning and washing up in a hotel.

5 An employee develops skills through the training process, both on-the-job and off-the-job.

6 **Piece rate** is paid according to the number of units of output produced by an employee. **Time rate** is paid according to the number of minutes or hours worked by an employee.
Time rate is more appropriate where the employee needs to take care over their work and not rush and make errors, e.g. in nursing. **Piece rate** is suitable when the employee needs to maintain a rate of output and where there is little chance of error as a result of speedier work, e.g. in routine work such as stuffing envelopes.

7 **Profit-sharing** means that employees receive rewards in proportion to the profits made by the company. This encourages efforts in line with company objectives.

8 **Commission** is given to encourage salespeople to increase the number of sales they make. It is a reward for their efforts and skill in selling.

9 **Fringe benefits** include luncheon vouchers, a company car, discounts on company products and company payment of telephone bills.

10 An electrical components manufacturer may pay **bonuses** at times when it is important to increase or maintain productivity, e.g. when the firm has an important order to meet, or in the period leading up to the Christmas and/or summer holiday.

11 **Compulsory deductions** from the pay packet include income tax and national insurance contributions. Possible **voluntary deductions** include trade union subscriptions, private pension contributions and contributions to health insurance schemes.

12 **Job analysis** is important to identify exactly what a new job will involve.

13 A **job description** describes a job of work. It includes details such as the title of the job, the main purposes of the job, the responsibilities of the job-holder, the type of decisions that the job-holder will need to make, and any responsibility for resources.

14 A **job description** helps the new job-holder to know exactly what they are expected to do and what their responsibilities are. If they are uncertain, they can check in their job

description. Job descriptions are useful in settling disputes over terms of employment.

15 The **job advertisement** should identify the job title; the location of the job; where to apply; the salary or wage; any fringe benefits, and give a brief description of key features of the job.

16 In planning a **job interview** it is important to decide on the questions to be asked and to make sure they fit in with the company's Equal Opportunities policy. Other issues are: the room layout; who will ask what questions and in what order; the timing of the interview; and the criteria for selecting the successful candidate.

17 A **person specification** goes beyond the job description to set out the mental and physical requirements of the job-holder.

18 **Internal training** is carried out in-house – i.e. within the company itself, rather than in a college or other external training establishment. Internal training can be geared specifically to meet the needs of a company; it is cheap to run, and easy to evaluate in terms of an organisation's objectives.

19 **External training** involves company employees taking part in courses run by outside training agencies. The advantage is that trainees can draw on skills and expertise that are not available within the company itself; this helps the company to introduce new ideas and innovations.

20 Training is both a **cost** and a **benefit**. It is a cost in that the company must pay for it, both in terms of time and other resources. The benefit is that it adds to the vitality, motivation and skills of the people who work for the company.

21 **Induction** is the period in which someone learns how to fit into an organisation for the first time. They often 'learn the ropes' by visiting people and departments within the company to find out what is going on and to learn about key issues such as Health and Safety.

22 **Career development** is the process by which company employees develop themselves and their skills. It is concerned with enabling people to fulfil their own learning and work needs so that they become better members of the organisation and more capable of taking on further work and responsibilities. It is important both to the person being developed and to the organisation.

23 Ideally, training should take place throughout the time an employee works for a company, from induction right through to retirement. It is particularly important when new initiatives are being introduced in the workplace or when an individual is taking on new responsibilities.

24 The **training gap** is the difference between an individual's current levels of skills and competence and what they are capable of. It can also be thought of as the gap between existing skills and potential skills.

25 Today organisations are continually changing and updating. Employees need to be able to cope with this dynamic age by continually retraining and developing new work skills – it is a process of lifelong learning.

Section 5: Aiding and Controlling Business Activity

Show That You Know It! page 65

1 Government supports business by:
   a) subsidising certain activities e.g. some aspects of farming
   b) protecting businesses against unfair competition
   c) by fining and penalising businesses that create social costs such as pollution which adversely affect other businesses
   d) by helping to build infrastructure (e.g. roads, motorways, etc.) which

help businesses to be more competitive

   e) by boosting the economy through its own expenditure in times of recession, etc.

2 **Competition policy** helps business by trying to create a 'level playing field' which encourages competition. It seeks to stop firms from becoming too large and having a dominant position in the market. It also seeks to prevent agreements between companies which are harmful to the interests of other businesses and consumers.

3 Government controls business activity through taxation, subsidy of activities, fines, laws setting standards and requirements, by direct intervention (e.g. the ownership of public corporations) and by setting the macro-economic climate in the economy (i.e. pumping more or less money into the economy through government spending). **Taxes** are used to discourage certain activities as well as to raise revenue for the government. E.g. taxes on cigarettes and spirits have the effect of reducing the consumption of these products while also generating revenue for the government.

4 The government needs to intervene because the economy may not run smoothly when left to its own devices. There are certain imperfections in the market and market failures. An example is the **monopoly power** which some firms enjoy, enabling them to exploit consumers and to take unfair advantage over rivals. The government also intervenes to protect weaker members of society e.g. by providing state pensions and a National Health Service. The government can also intervene for political reasons, e.g. to tax the rich and redistribute wealth to the poor.

5 **EU regulations** are binding in law on member states. They are drafted by EU commissioners and are approved by the Council of Ministers and the European Parliament. Once a regulation is adopted by the Council of Ministers, it is binding in its entirety and applicable as it stands to all member states, including the UK.

6 A good example of a government policy is the decision to curb the expansion of road building programmes in the UK in line with European and international environmental policies. One of the effects of this is likely to be greater traffic congestion in some parts of the UK. This will either raise business costs or lead to the relocation of businesses to areas where existing communication links are of a good standard.

7 Farmers may be affected by government regulation and activity in the choice of crops and livestock they grow and rear. Farmers will channel their resources into those lines which yield the highest returns – i.e. often those with the greatest levels of subsidy. Farmers are affected by taxes on profits in that this acts as a cost of production. Farmers keep a keen eye on the level of support given to agriculture because ultimately their livelihoods depend on it. When the government encourages economic activity, e.g. by lowering taxes, this encourages farmers because they know that national spending is likely to rise.

   A small shopkeeper's livelihood depends on the general level of spending in the economy. If the government encourages expansion this will benefit the small shopkeeper. The shopkeeper is also affected by taxation, particularly business rates levied by the local authority.

8 Government encourages businesses to move to areas of high unemployment by offering **regional incentives**, e.g. subsidies, grants and 'tax holidays'. Local government may also build factory units and roads to encourage firms to set up in areas of higher-than-average unemployment.

9 Trade union aims in a car plant may be

to ensure good wages for employees in comparison to the industry average, and to secure good social arrangements, including favourable holiday allowances and hours of work.

10 If formal negotiation fails, the union may suggest some form of **conciliation or arbitration** by an independent third party. Alternatively, the union can resort to official industrial action, by holding a strike, work-to-rule or go-slow, effectively withdrawing the co-operation of the workforce.

11 **ACAS is an independent body which seeks to help management and employees to arrive at mutually beneficial solutions to industrial problems.**

12 **Health and Safety** is the responsibility of both the individual employee *and* of the employer. Health and Safety is supervised by the Health and Safety Executive and its Inspectorate.

13 **RIDDOR**, the Reporting of Injuries, Diseases and Dangerous Occurrences Regulations, require the reporting of accidents in the workplaces, as well as listed diseases and accidents involving work equipment.
    COSHH – the Control of Substances Hazardous to Health regulations – state that employers must identify work tasks which are likely to be harmful and take steps to minimise the risks. Training must be given to employees who work with such substances.

14 A **contract of employment** becomes binding in law as soon as an employer has verbally agreed to employ a worker and the worker has accepted that employment. The contract of employment will include the job title, the date of commencement of employment, holiday entitlement, hours of work, the period of notice that must be given, and the rate and method of pay.

15 The four key areas covered by **Equal Opportunities** legislation are sex discrimination, race relations, equal pay and disabled workers' rights.

16 The **Disabled Workers Act** states that firms employing over 20 people must include at least 3% disabled people among their workforce.

17 **Direct discrimination** involves clear cases of discrimination where one person is favoured rather than another on grounds of sex, race, religion, etc.
    Indirect discrimination is less obvious, being based on requirements which can be more easily be met by people of a particular sex, race, religion, etc. than by other groups – e.g. the requirement that employees must wear safety helmets might indirectly discriminate against Sikhs.

18 An example of indirect discrimination might be the requirement that employees work on certain days when particular ethnic groups observe religious holidays.

19 The **Race Relations Act** protects against discrimination on racial, religious, and ethnic grounds.

20 An employee may claim **unfair dismissal** if they have been dismissed for being pregnant, where this factor is irrelevant to their work performance. An employee can also claim unfair dismissal if they are sacked for their union activities.

21 A **law** is created externally to an organisation or industry by the legal authorities in a country, e.g. by Act of Parliament. A **voluntary code of practice** is usually established by firms operating in a particular industry and is a form of self-policing.

22 The **Sale of Goods Act** states that goods must be 'free from significant defects' – i.e. fit for the intended purpose; the **Trades Descriptions Act** states that the description of a particular good or service must be accurate.

23 The **Food Safety Act** is concerned with making sure that food is prepared in a safe and appropriate way, e.g. in hotels and restaurants.

24 The local authority's **Trading Standards Department** investigates local consumer issues, such as the false description of goods and the accuracy of weights and measures.

25 The **Environmental Health Department** is responsible for inspecting premises such as food shops and restaurants in order to make sure that food is being stored and prepared in a safe way.

Test Yourself in Exam Conditions

A Corporate Gift, page 67

1 You will get two marks for each point that you are able to develop, e.g.:

> Peter will benefit from moving to London because of the larger market (*1 mark*) that exists, particularly with the many large firms in the area (*1 mark*).

> Peter will be able to keep down his costs (*1 mark*) by being located close to his final customers, reducing the cost of transport and time wasted (*1 mark*).

Other relevant answers would also enable you to score up to 2 marks for points which are well developed.

2 You will get up to 2 marks for developing a disadvantage, e.g.:

> Peter's costs such as rent and rates will be higher (*1 mark*) close to London because of the demand for space in prime business locations (*1 mark*).

Other relevant answers would be accepted.

3 Up to 2 marks for defining opportunity cost:

> Opportunity cost is the next-best alternative sacrificed by Peter (*1 mark*) in making his decision to set up in business (*1 mark*).

Up to 2 marks for explaining the opportunity cost to Peter – the real cost might be the wages he could have earnt (*1 mark*) if he had decided to work for someone else (*1 mark*).

4 Up to 3 marks for explaining the benefits of being a private company rather than a sole trader, e.g.:

> As a private company Peter would be able to raise more capital (*1 mark*) by selling shares (*1 mark*). He would also have limited liability (*1 mark*).

Three further marks for applying the answer specifically to the case study e.g.:

> As a producer of corporate gifts Peter would require large sums of capital (*1 mark*) which would not be available to a one-person business (*1 mark*). Because Peter is located close to London, the running costs of the business would be high, necessitating a sizeable injection of capital(*1 mark*).

Other appropriate answers would also be accepted.

5 This question simply asks you to explain niche marketing. Up to 3 marks are given for the development of an accurate explanation of niche marketing, e.g.:

> A niche is one part of a larger market (*1 mark*), the niche market having specific characteristics which make it different from the wider market (*1 mark*). A firm

could position its product offer so that it appeals to the particular niche that it has identified (*1 mark*).

6 One mark for each element of the marketing mix identified, i.e. Price, Place, Product and Promotion (maximum of 2 marks for listing elements of the marketing mix). Two further marks for each development of an aspect of the marketing mix. E.g. for price:

Peter felt that he could produce more expensive corporate gifts (*1 mark*) because this would enable corporate buyers to feel that they were getting a more upmarket product (*1 mark*).

E.g. Promotion:

Peter was able to promote his products by making personal visits to clients (*1 mark*) and by writing to relevant people within the organisations he wanted to deal with and enclosing a mailshot (*1 mark*).

7 One mark for each relevant alternative source of finance identified, e.g. overdraft, and a mortgage. Three marks for development of each type of finance and application to the example of Corporoclocks, e.g.:

Corporoclocks could have taken out an overdraft rather than a loan because the interest payable would be limited to the amount overdrawn at any one moment in time (*1 mark*). This could prove to be a cheaper method of short-term finance (*1 mark*) because Peter could have made a clear cash flow budget anticipating flows of money into and out of the bank. Corporoclocks might have decided to purchase their premises (*1 mark*) by means of a mortgage which could be paid back over 20 to 25 years (*1 mark*) thus spreading the cost of premises, and the premises would eventually be owned by the business (*1 mark*).

8 Three marks for explaining the impact of an increase in interest rates. Three marks for explaining the impact of a fall in interest rates, e.g:

If interest rates rise, this would raise the cost to Corporoclocks of borrowing money (*1 mark*). Also consumers (i.e. corporate clients) would have less money to spend on Corporoclock products (*1 mark*), probably leading to a fall in orders (*1 mark*). When interest rates fall it becomes easier and cheaper for Corporoclocks to borrow money (*1 mark*); also corporations are more inclined to borrow money (*1 mark*) and buy more corporate gifts, which will benefit Corporoclock's sales.

9 a) Up to 2 marks for each development of a feature of an advertisement in the local press – up to 8 marks maximum, e.g. title of the job clearly set out at top of advertisement; location of post; pay rates; hours of work; who to apply to in the company, e.g. Personnel Manager; address of Corporoclocks, and brief job description.

b) Up to 2 marks for each development of component of the job description., to include elements such as title of the post; the main purposes of the job; supervisory responsibilities; types of decision to be made; responsibilities of the post-holder for resources.

c) Up to 3 marks for each aspect of planning the interview. Third mark to be given in each case only if the aspect is related to the specific job of part-time secretary. Aspects to be covered include planning the questions; deciding who is to ask what; giving the candidate opportunities to ask questions, etc.

10 **a)** Six marks for stating that the break-even point would be 400 clocks. Students could score 6 marks for drawing an accurate break-even chart with correctly labelled axes showing Sales and Total Cost. Alternatively students could get up to 6 marks by using the formula that Break-even = Fixed Costs divided by Contribution per clock.

   b) Two marks for stating that 1,200 clocks would generate £30,000 of sales, which would cost £14,000 to produce (£8,000 of fixed costs and £6,000 of variable costs).

   c) Up to 3 marks for accurately defining cash flow forecasting as involving projections (*1 mark*) of likely future inflows of cash in and out of the company (*1 mark*), revealing possible periods of shortfall. An extra 3 marks for specifically relating this information to Corporoclocks.

11 Up to 3 marks for a general explanation of the process of market research, e.g. by carrying out field research; sending out questionnaires to potential clients (*1 mark*); and then analysing the results in a quantitative way (*1 mark*); or by carrying out more detailed qualitative research to investigate small numbers of clients and their preferences. Three extra marks for application of the answer directly to Corporoclocks and its customers.

12 Three marks for the development of each appropriate point, e.g.:

   Corporoclocks might segment its market according to the industrial sector (*1 mark*) that its clients are operating in, e.g. oil, textiles, etc (*1 mark*), because clients in these sectors may have substantial similarities which make them different from other sectors (*1 mark*). Other types of segmentation could include geographical region, country of origin, size and turnover of company, etc.

13 Up to 2 marks for each appropriate point developed, e.g.:

   A small company is able to develop personal relationships (*1 mark*) with each of its clients based on an ongoing personalised dialogue (*1 mark*). A small company is more flexible (*1 mark*) and able to respond more quickly to changes in the marketplace (*1 mark*). A small company can keep its costs down (*1 mark*) by focusing on what it does best (*1 mark*).

   Maximum of 5 marks for this question.

14 One mark for listing an item, and 1 additional mark for describing it, e.g.:

   Premises – the physical buildings owned by an organisation

   Stocks – goods waiting to be sold

   Cash – liquid cash waiting to be converted into other assets

1   a) Up to 6 marks for accurately plotting and labelling the break-even chart. One mark for accurate Total Revenue line, 1 mark for accurate Total Cost line, 1 mark for accurate Fixed Cost line, 1 mark for drawing in break-even point. One mark for accurately labelling the two axes.

    b) 400 sandwiches per day (*2 marks*)

2   a) 1 mark for one fixed cost, 2 marks for 2 fixed costs – rent of the premises and business rates.

    b) 1 mark each for 2 accurate variable costs, e.g. labour and electricity. e.g. bread and fillings.

3   Two marks for each developed point, e.g.:

Super Sandwiches produces in batches because there is not enough demand (*1 mark*) to focus on just producing one line of sandwich (*1 mark*).

By producing in batches it is possible to concentrate (*1 mark*) on one type of batch and its ingredients and processes at a time (*1 mark*).

4   a) 1 mark for each feature of a partnership (maximum 2), e.g.:

… Consists of at least two people (*1 mark*); usually set up by Deed of Partnership (*1 mark*); has unlimited liability (*1 mark*) etc.

    b) Up to 3 marks for each appropriate advantage of a limited company, e.g.:

Company status would provide limited liability (*1 mark*) enabling the owners of the company to have their own personal possessions protected against business debts (*1 mark*), encouraging more people to put capital into the business (*1 mark*).

A private company makes it possible to employ specialist managers (*1 mark*) whose skills and expertise (*1 mark*) may be more extensive than those of the partners.

5   a) and b)
One mark for choosing an appropriate way of financing the cost. Two further marks for giving reasons why method is suitable, e.g.:

Electricity costs could be financed by credit payment (*1 mark*); the firm would use the electricity and pay at the end of the quarter. This would enable them to use the electricity to make sandwiches (*1 mark*) which could then be sold and turned into cash, enabling later payment of the bill (*1 mark*).

The cost of machinery and equipment could be financed by a leasing arrangement (*1 mark*) whereby the sandwich company never actually owns the machinery but leases it out. Super Sandwiches would not have to worry about the depreciation (*1 mark*) on the equipment it uses, nor would it have to worry about servicing the equipment (*1 mark*).

6   a) Two marks for describing the primary sector of the economy as being involved in the extraction (*1 mark*) of the gifts of nature (*1 mark*).

    b) Up to 2 marks for showing how super sandwiches uses bread and fillings (*1 mark*) which are produced by agriculture and fisheries (*1 mark*).

    b) One mark for saying that Super Sandwiches is in the tertiary or services sector of the economy.

7   Up to two marks for explaining a business objective of Super

Sandwiches, e.g. profit maximisation, service, or market share.

8   **a)** Up to 3 marks for each developed argument for adopting a franchise structure, e.g.:

Super Sandwiches would be able to gain revenue (*1 mark*) from franchising its idea and name (*1 mark*) to a franchisee who would pay a lump sum and an ongoing share of the profits to trade under the Super Sandwiches name (*1 mark*).

By granting a franchise Super Sandwiches would have someone working for them (*1 mark*) who was also working for themselves (*1 mark*), creating a good recipe for motivation (*1 mark*) within the business.

   b) Up to 3 marks for each developed point, up to a maximum of 8. To gain the higher marks, each developed point must be related to Super Sandwiches, e.g.:

A franchisee benefits from trading under a well known name (*1 mark*), Super Sandwiches (*1 mark*), which is already recognised nationwide   (*1 mark*).

The franchisee is able to buy materials and equipment from Super Sandwiches (*1 mark*), which are tried and tested (*1 mark*) and proven to be successful in the Super Sandwiches business (*1 mark*).

The franchisee is able to get advice (*1 mark*) training (*1 mark*) and ongoing support from Super Sandwiches (*1 mark*).

9   Up to 2 marks for each appropriately developed point, e.g.:

The government creates legislation (*1 mark*) such as the Health and Safety at Work Act (*1 mark*) which

influences the way Super Sandwiches operates.

The government influences economic activity in the wider economy (*1 mark*) which helps to determine the level of demand for Super Sandwiches.

The government taxes (*1 mark*) the profits of companies like Super Sandwiches, which increases costs of production.

10   Up to 3 marks for each developed point appropriately supporting or criticising the advertisement, e.g.:

The advertisement gives too little detail (*1 mark*); there is no contact name (*1 mark*) on telephone number (*1 mark*).

The advertisement is not very visual (*1 mark*) and is unlikely to catch the eye (*1 mark*) when placed alongside more appealing advertisements giving more detail (*1 mark*).

11   Up to 4 marks for outlining details that would be in the job description, e.g. job title, responsibilities, decisions to be made, main purpose of job etc.
Two additional marks for clearly linking responses to Super Sandwiches and the job of part-time accountant.

12   Up to 3 marks for each appropriately developed argument outlining why Super Sandwiches would need to develop an induction programme for new employees, e.g.:

An induction programme should be designed to show new employees at Super Sandwiches the key features of what the job entails (*1 mark*), such as basic work processes (*1 mark*), and Health and Safety requirements of the job (*1 mark*).

The induction programme would enable new employees to meet other people (*1 mark*); to find out

about their responsibilities
(*1 mark*); and generally to reduce
any worries that they might have
about starting a new job (*1 mark*).

13 Up to 3 marks for each developed
argument which is related to Super
Sandwiches, e.g.:

Super Sandwiches would appeal to
a range of different customers
(*1 mark*), each group of whom
would be looking for something
different (*1 mark*). Super
Sandwiches should therefore try to
identify the characteristics and
requirements of each of these
segments (*1 mark*).

Super Sandwiches can maximise
revenue (*1 mark*) by providing
different offerings (*1 mark*) to
appeal to different income and taste
groupings (*1 mark*)

14 Up to 3 marks for identifying an
appropriate strategy related to each of
the four elements of the marketing
mix: Price, Product, Place and
Promotion. Only 4 marks maximum if
each element is simply listed. Only 8
marks maximum if each factor is listed
and explained but not related to Super
Sandwiches.

Up to 12 marks for evaluating each
strategy in relation to Super
Sandwiches.

15 Up to 2 marks for each explanation of
how a business like Super Sandwiches
could benefit from government
expenditure, e.g.:

Super Sandwiches could benefit
from a general rise in government
spending (*1 mark*); this would
generate a boom in expenditure
throughout the economy (*1 mark*).

Super Sandwiches could benefit
from a specific subsidy or grant
(*1 mark*) e.g. a start-up grant for
new businesses. (*1 mark*).